I0476608

How To Draw Star Wars : Pencil Drawings Step By Step

Pencil Drawing Ideas for Absolute Beginners

By Gala Publication

Published By:

Gala Publication

ISBN-13: 978- 1515213369
ISBN-10: 1515213366

©Copyright 2015 – Gala Publication

Table of Contents

Anakin

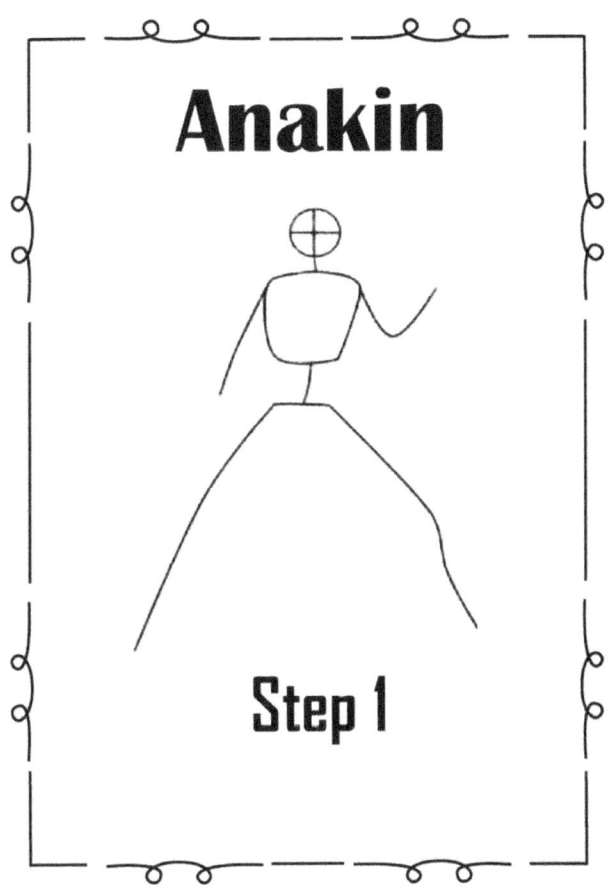

Step 1

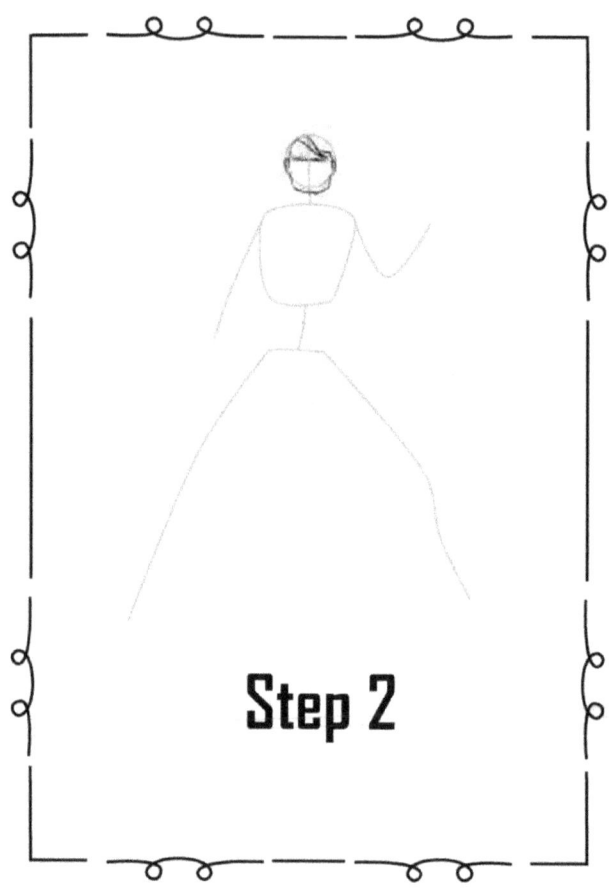

Step 2

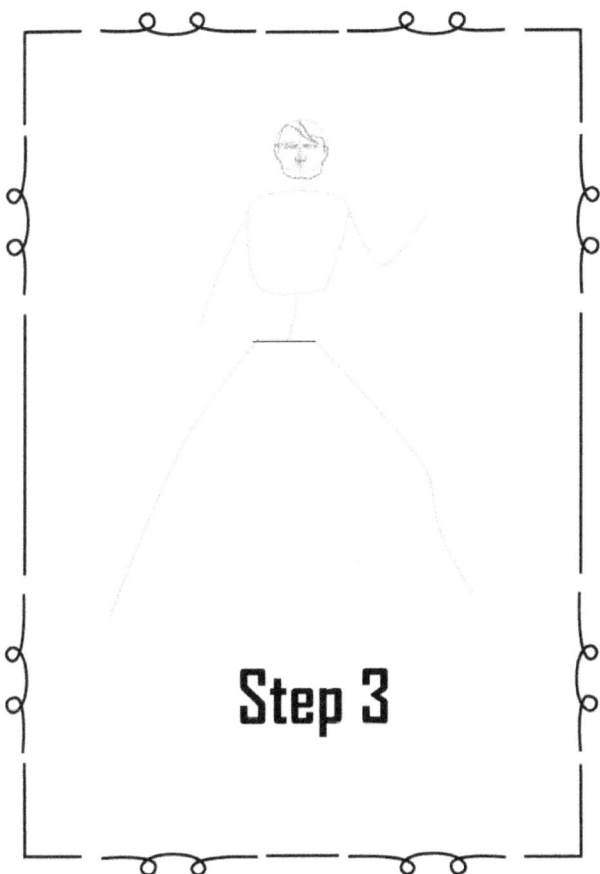

Step 3

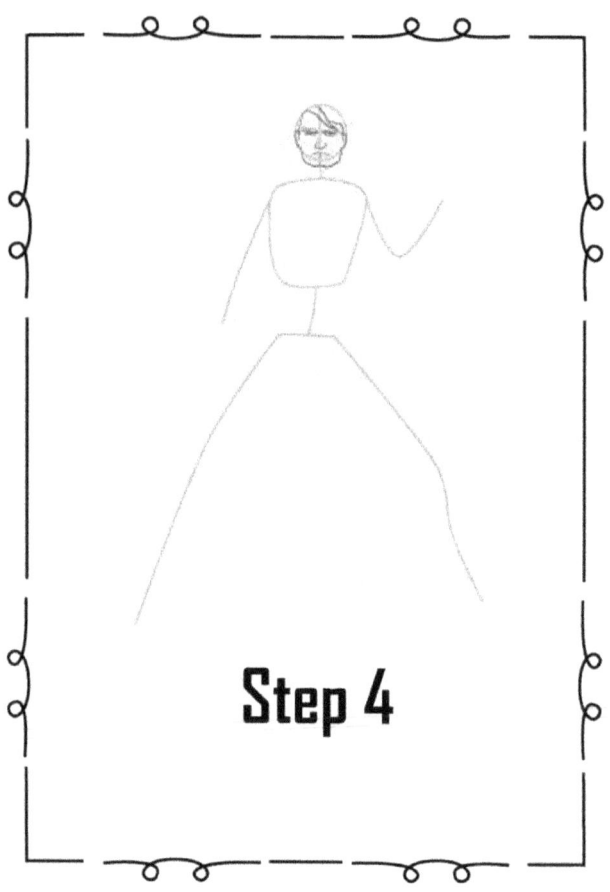

Step 4

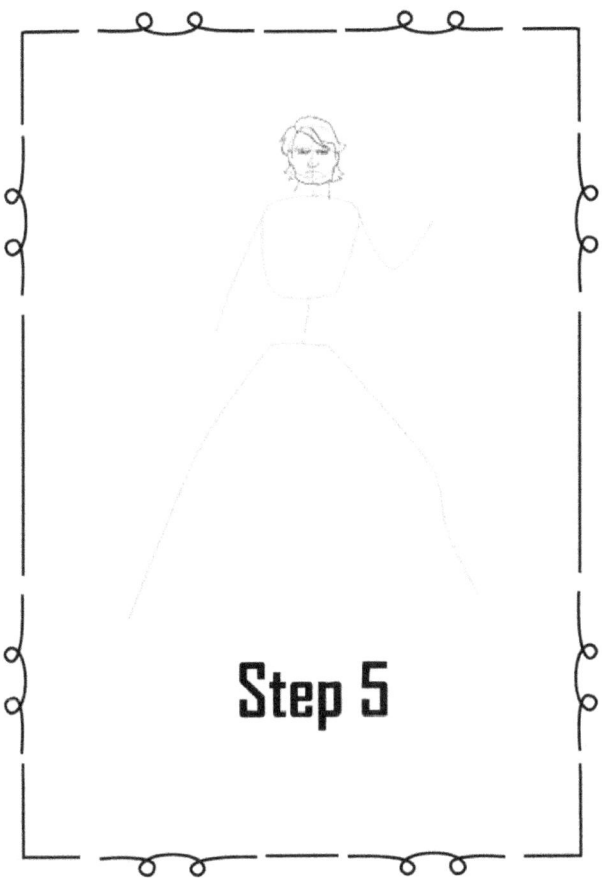

Step 5

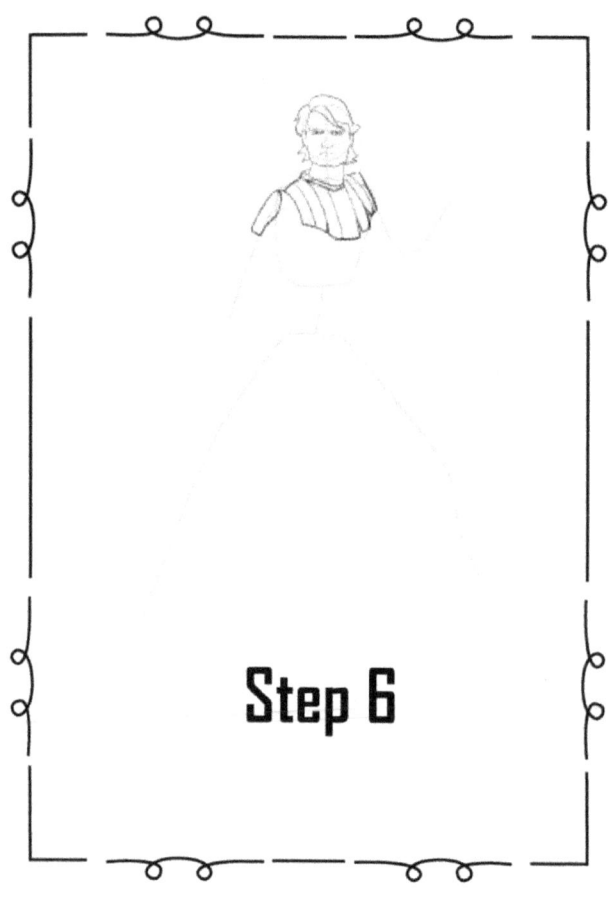

Step 6

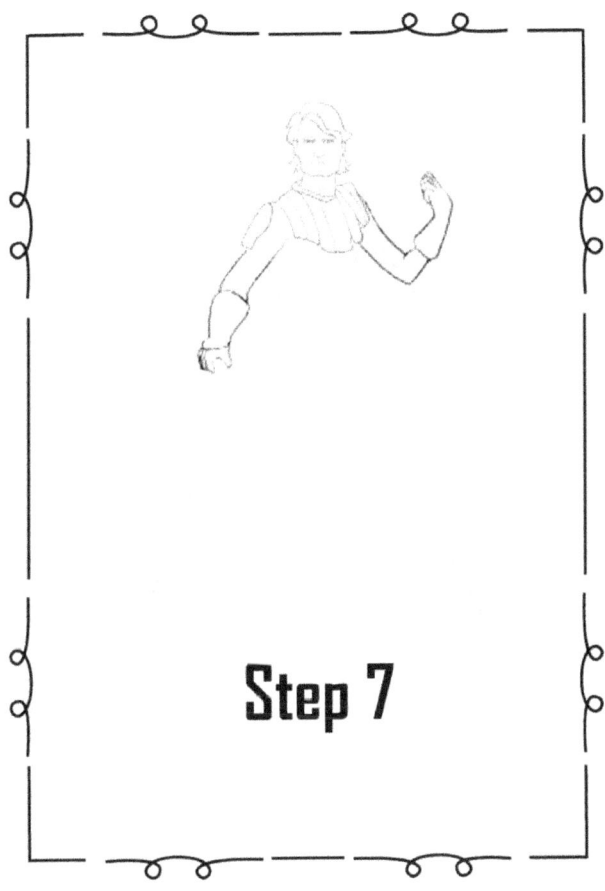

Step 7

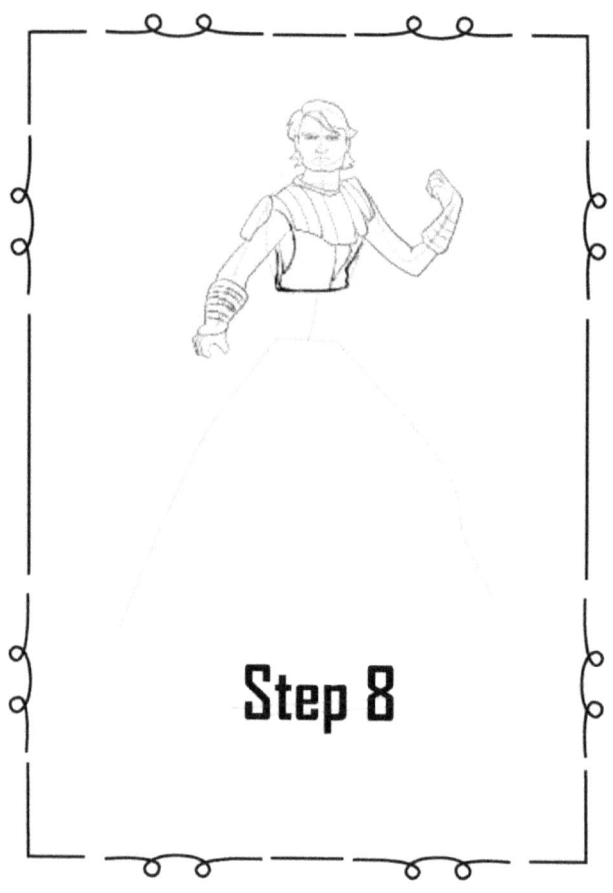

Step 8

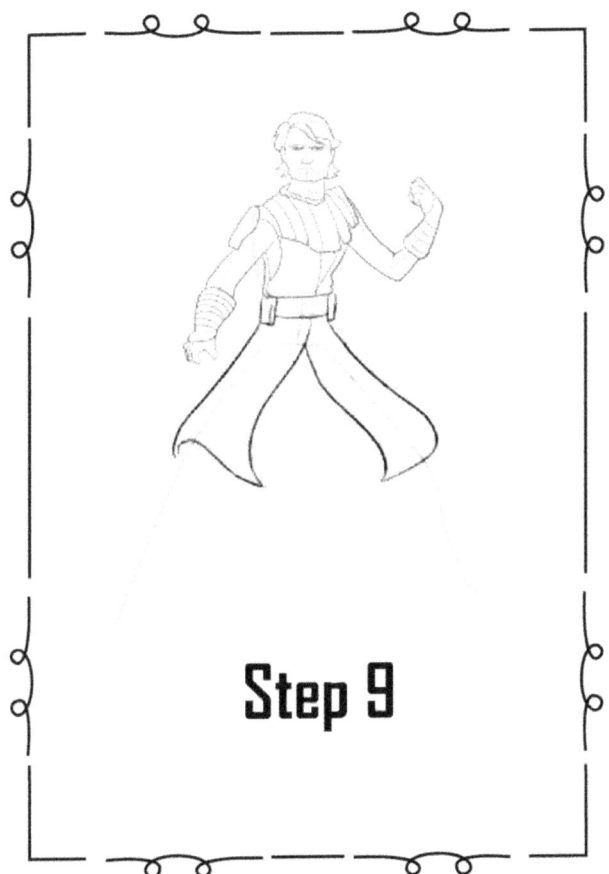

Step 9

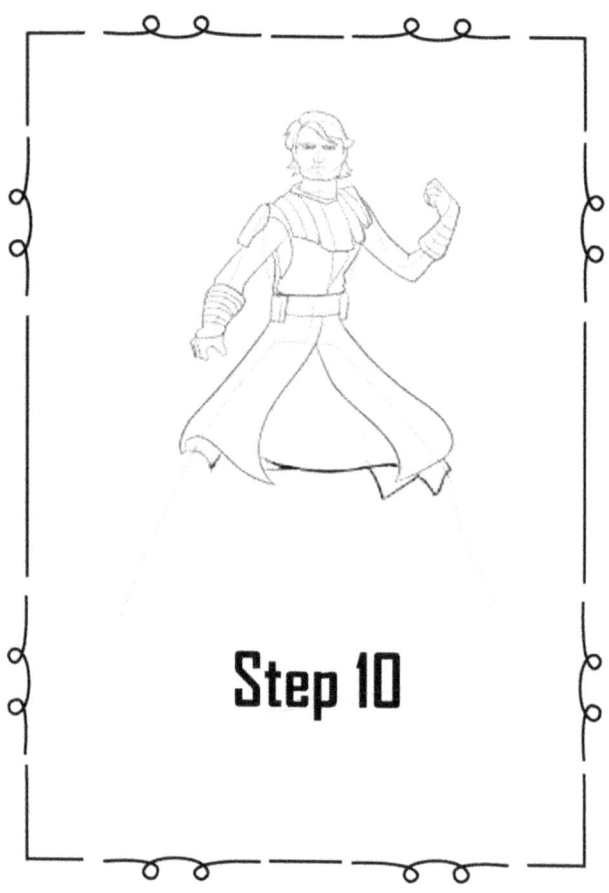

Step 10

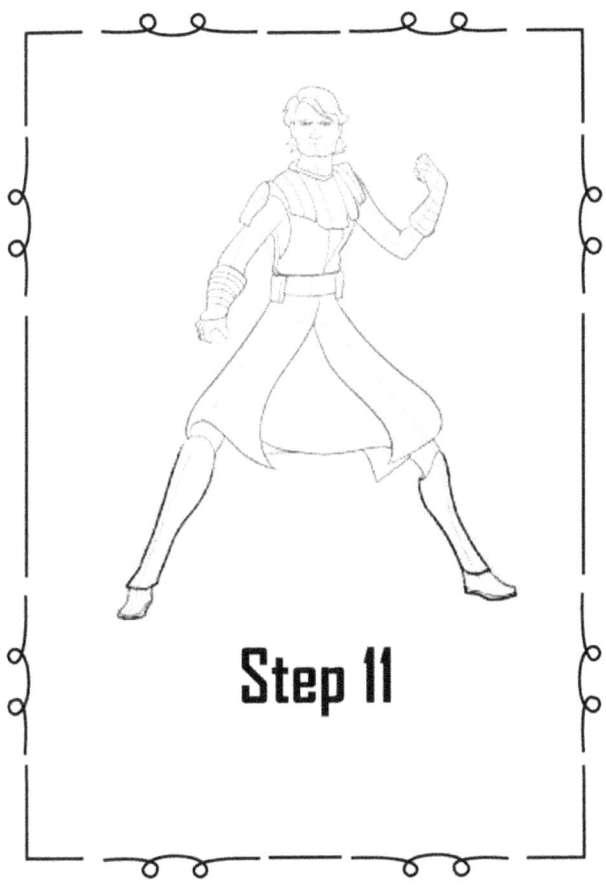

Step 11

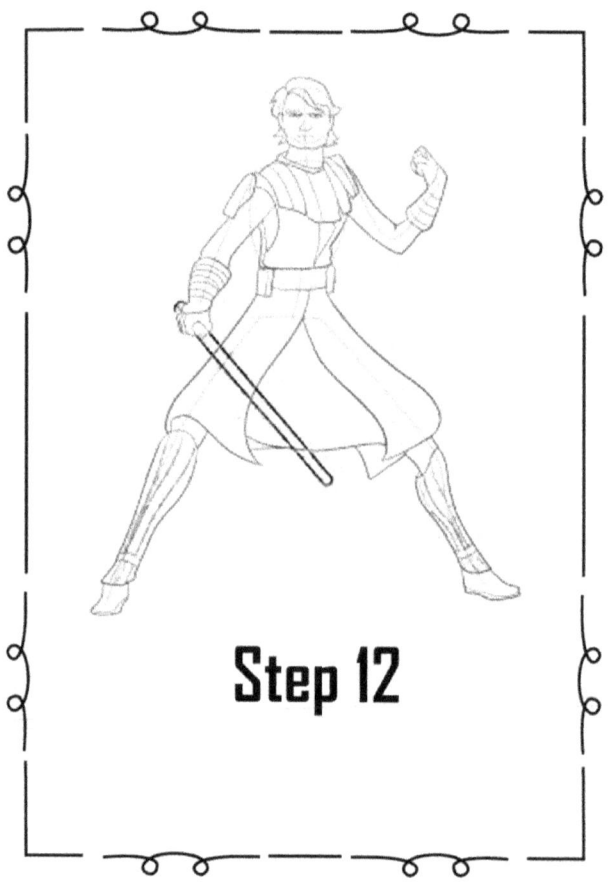

Step 12

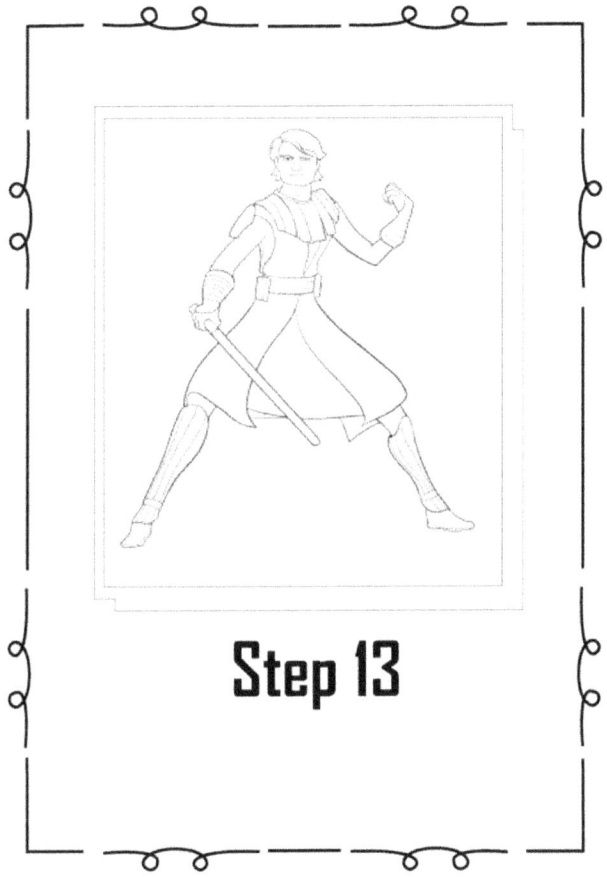

Step 13

Boba Fett

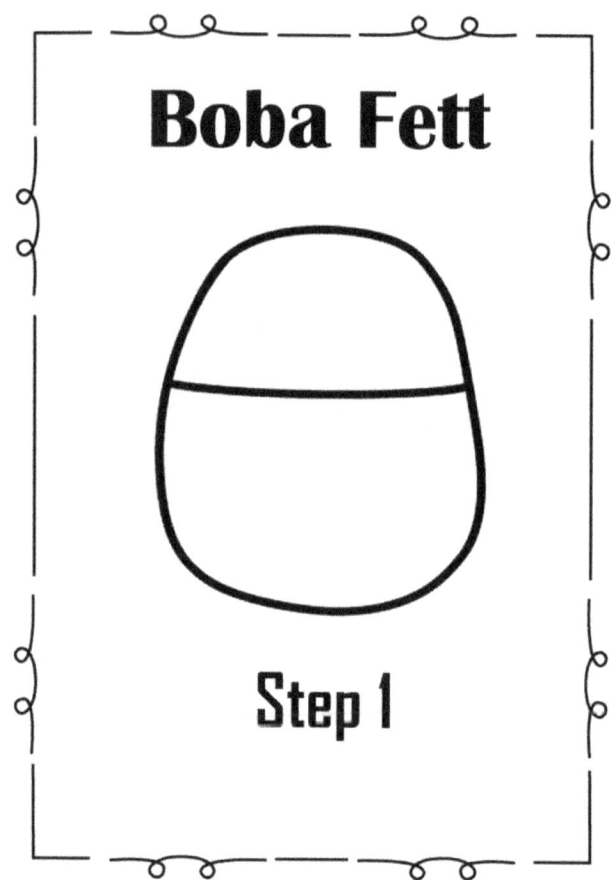

Step 1

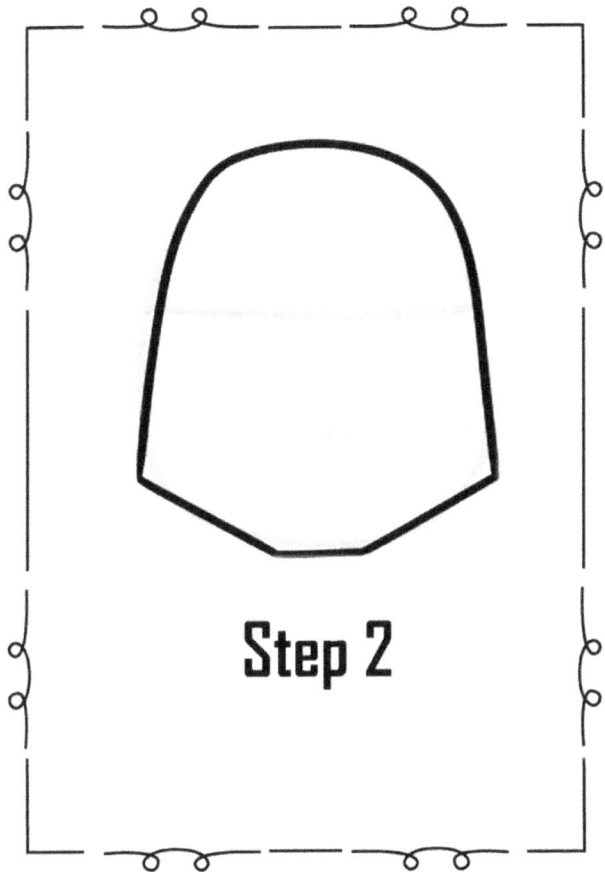

Step 2

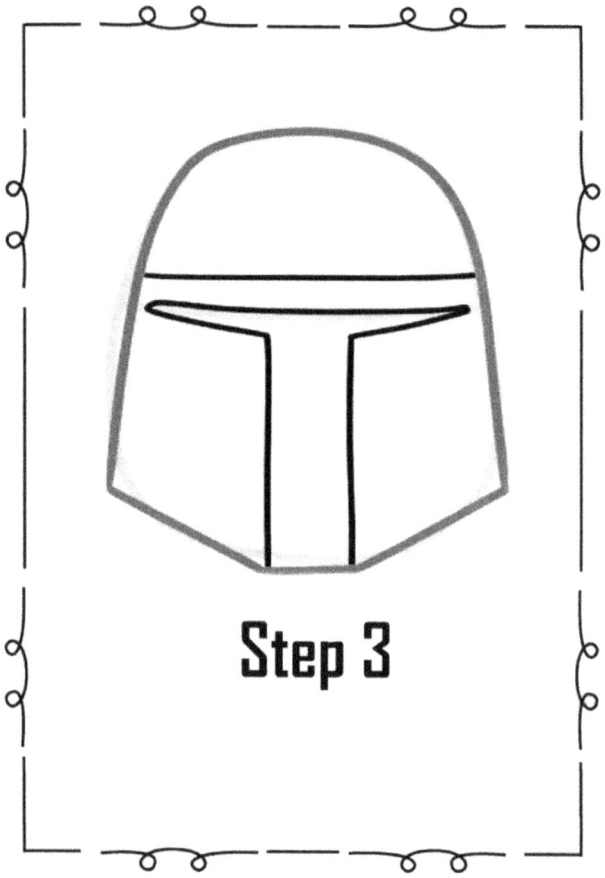

Step 3

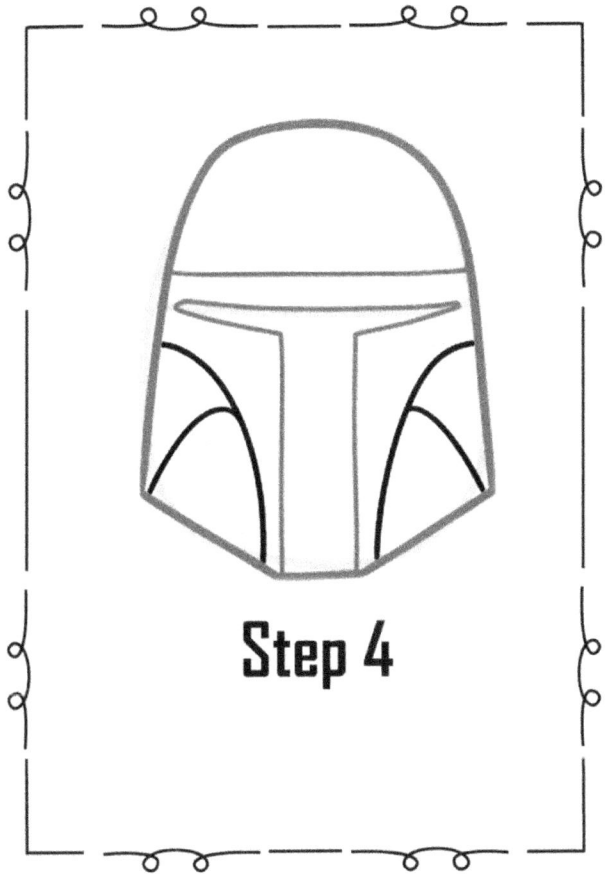

Step 4

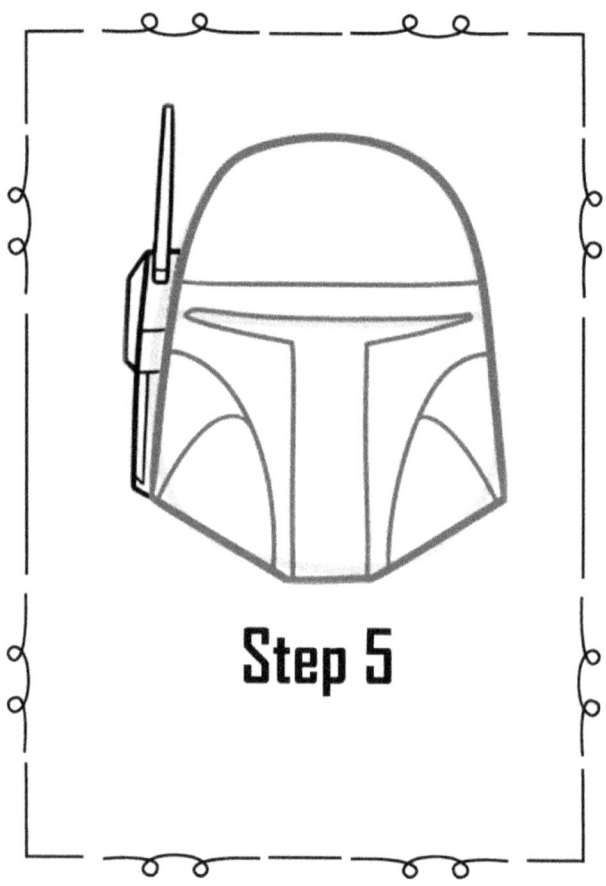

Step 5

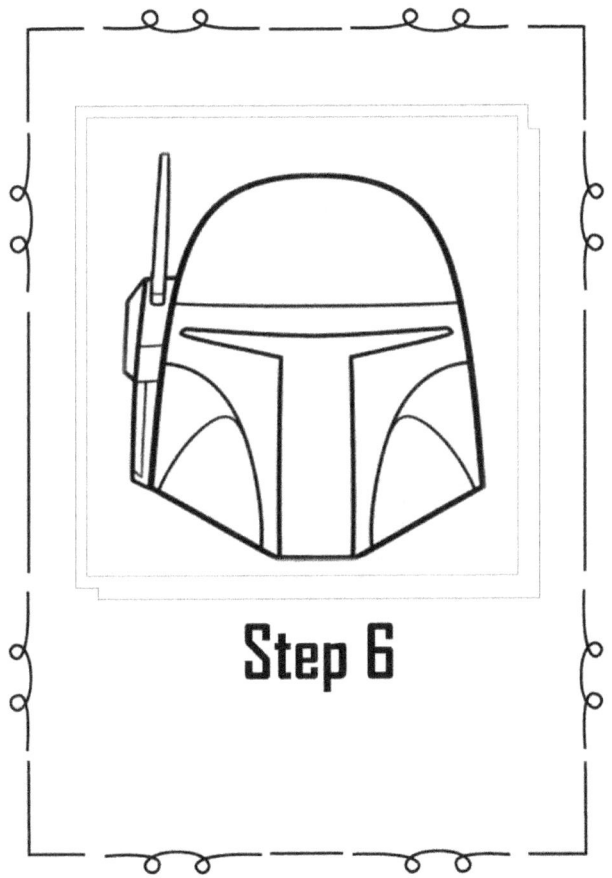

Step 6

Darth Vader

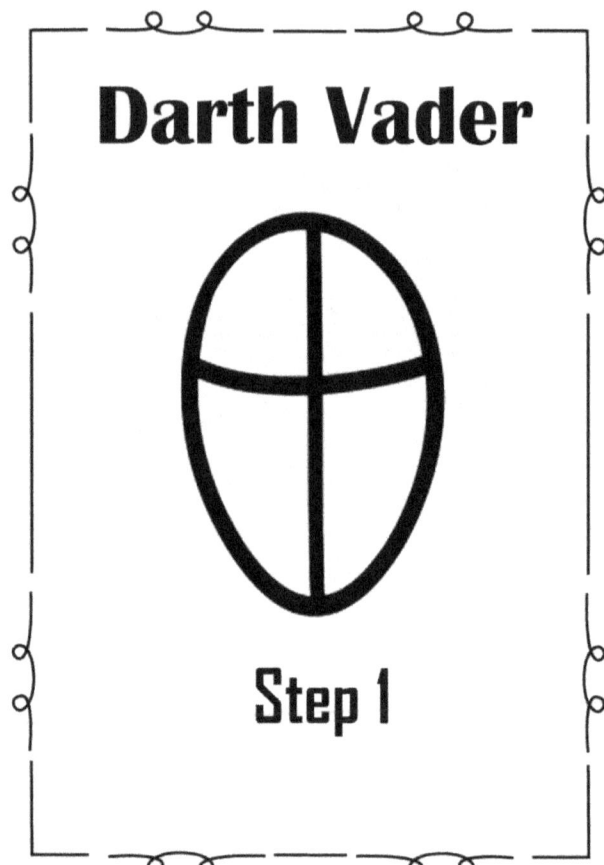

Step 1

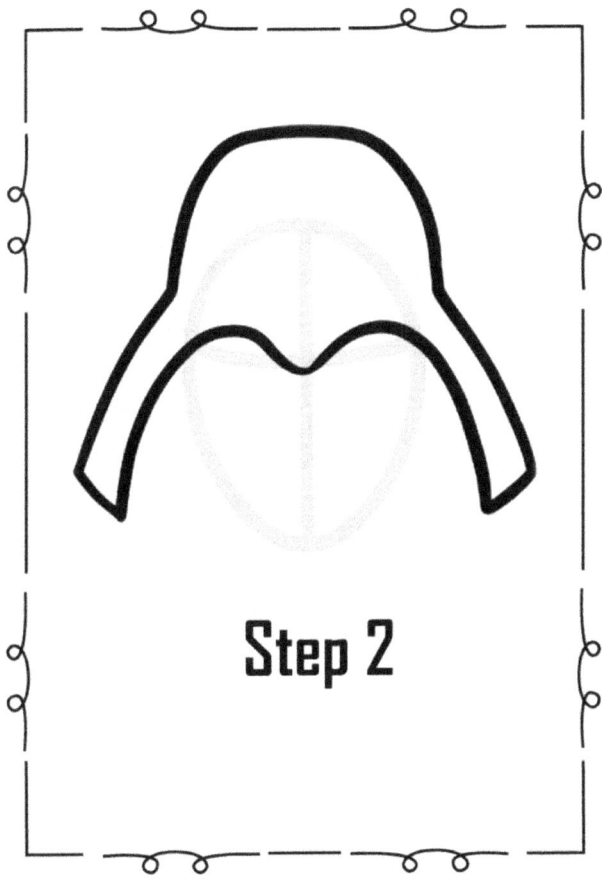

Step 2

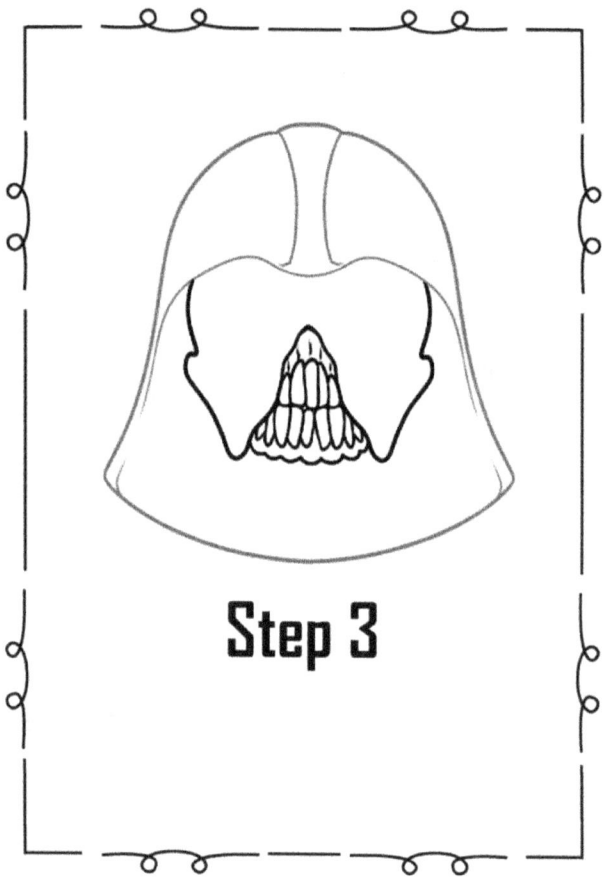

Step 3

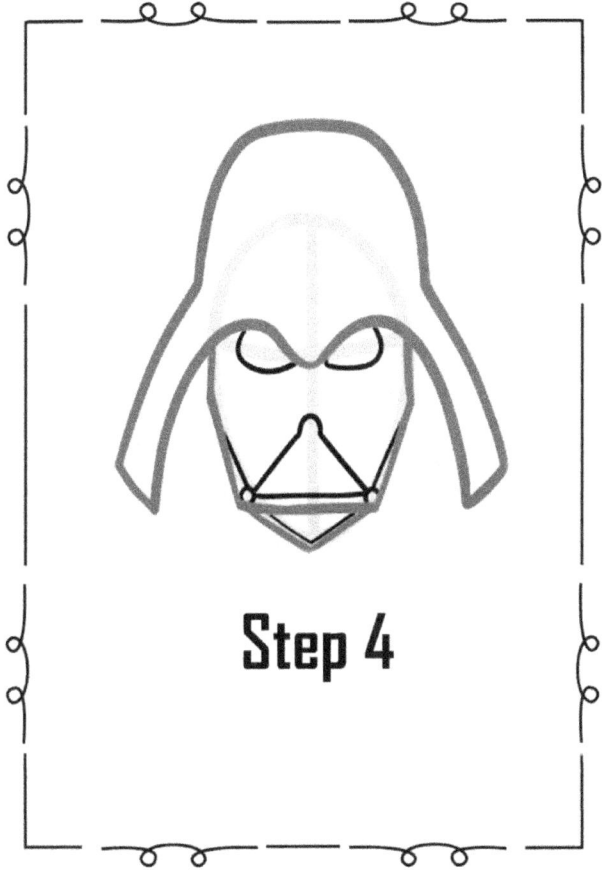

Step 4

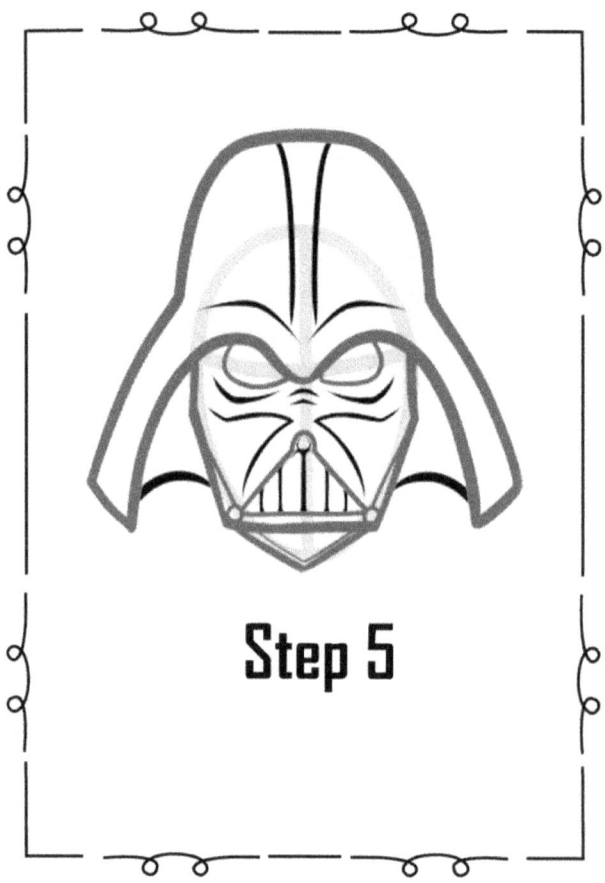

Step 5

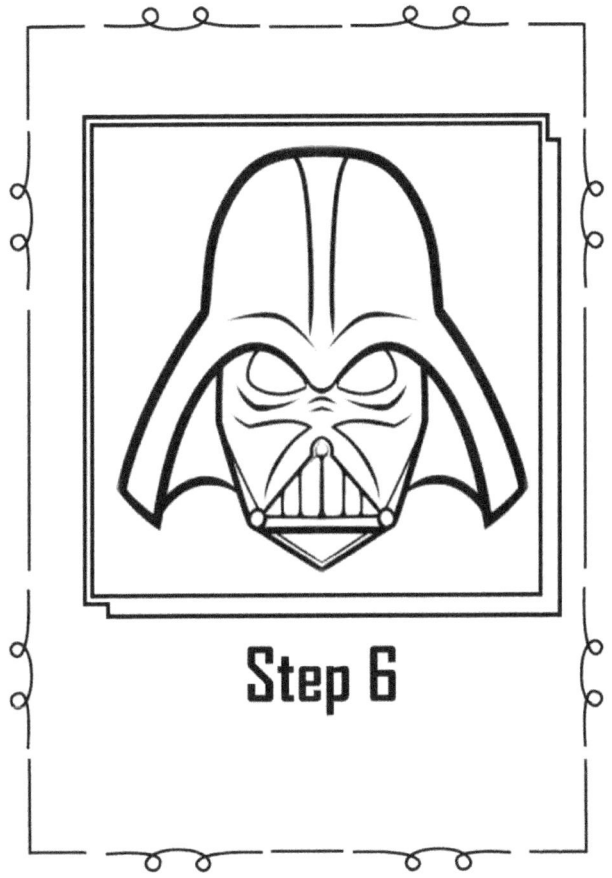

Step 6

Darth Vader Skull

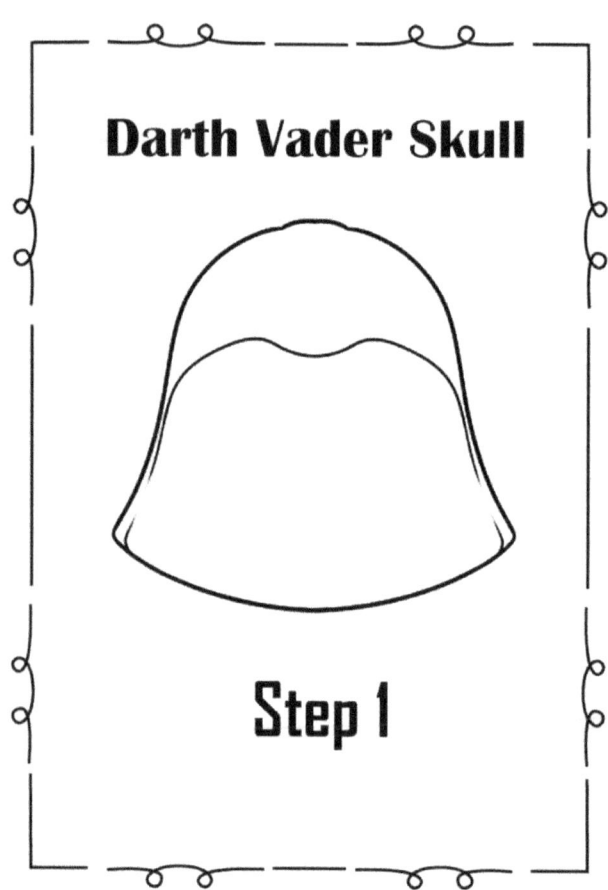

Step 1

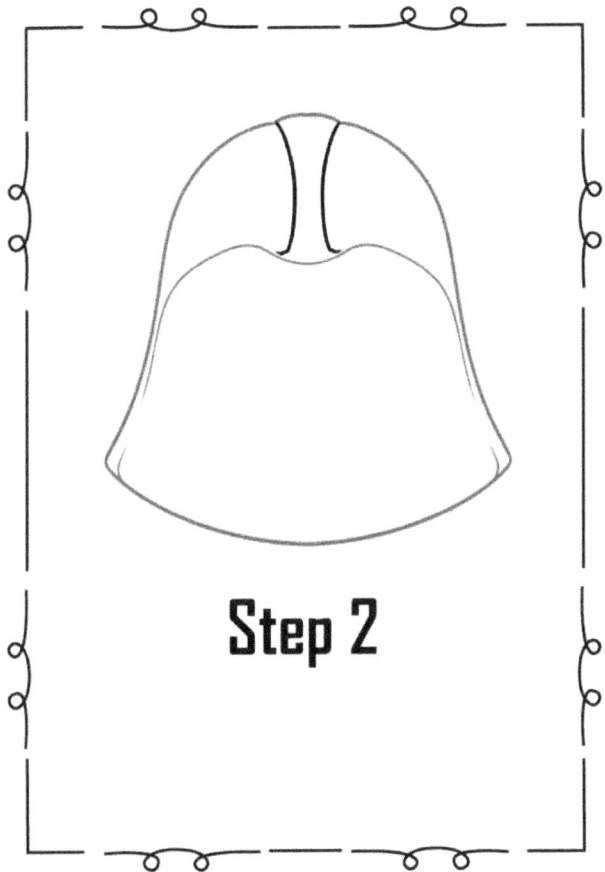

Step 2

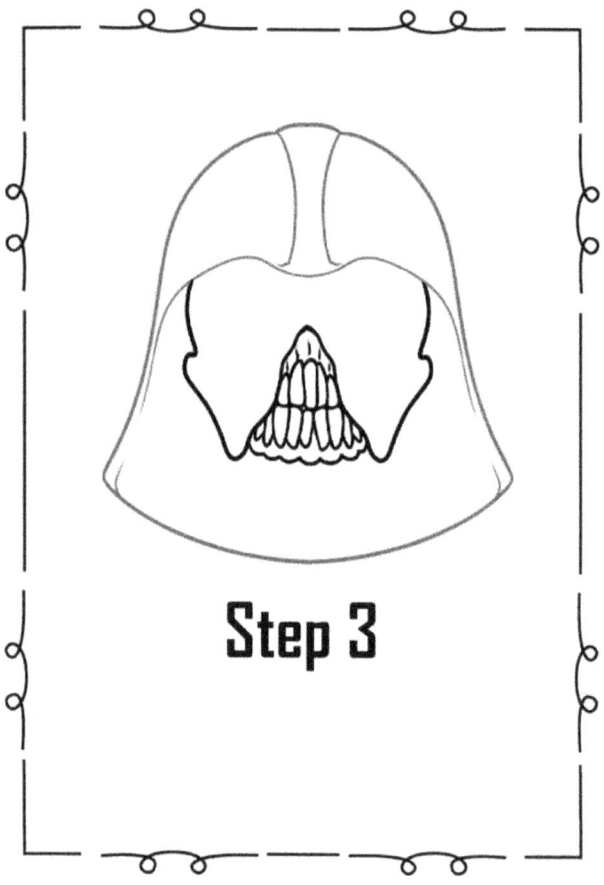

Step 3

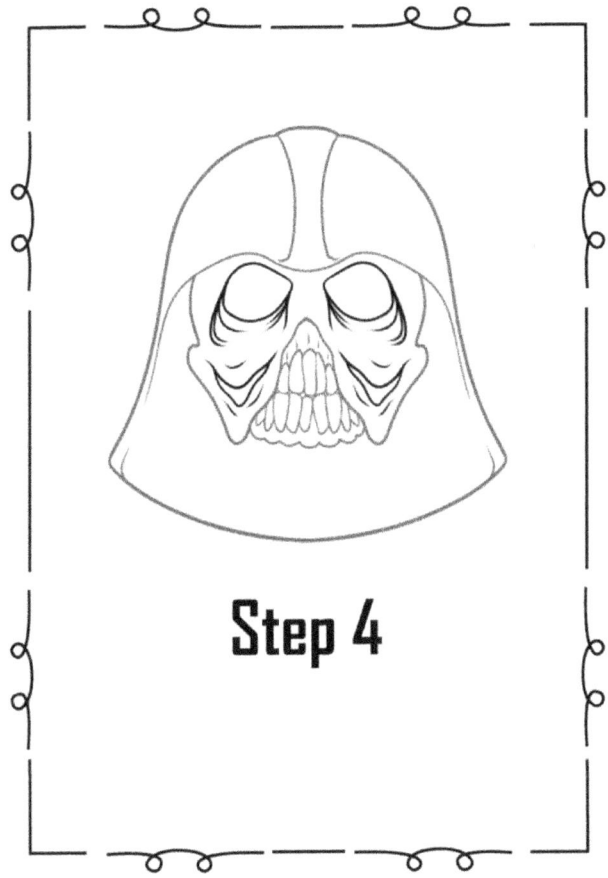

Step 4

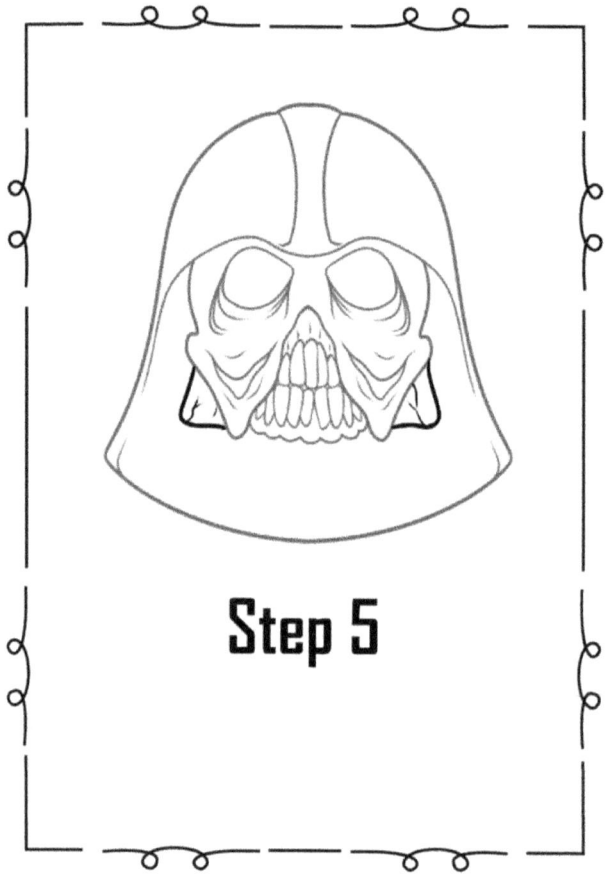

Step 5

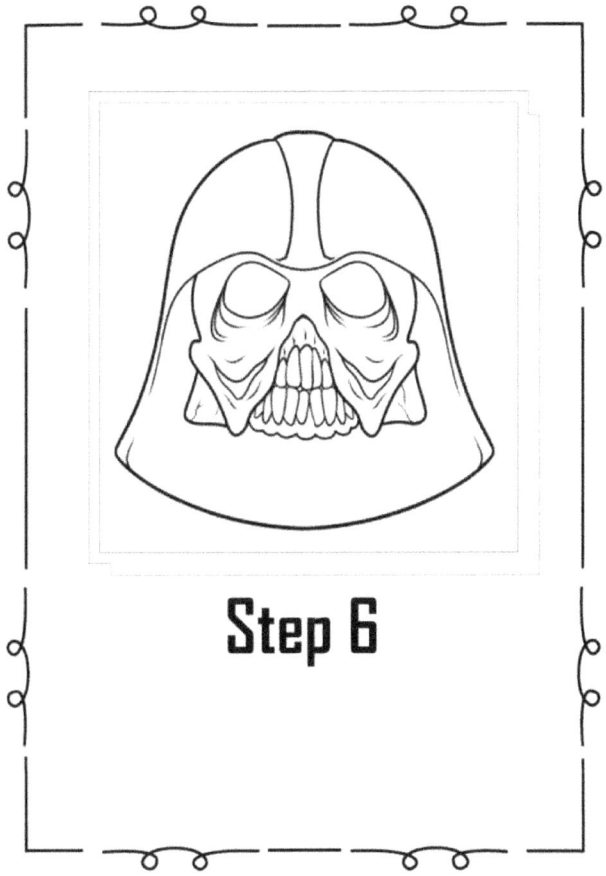

Step 6

Jabba the Hut

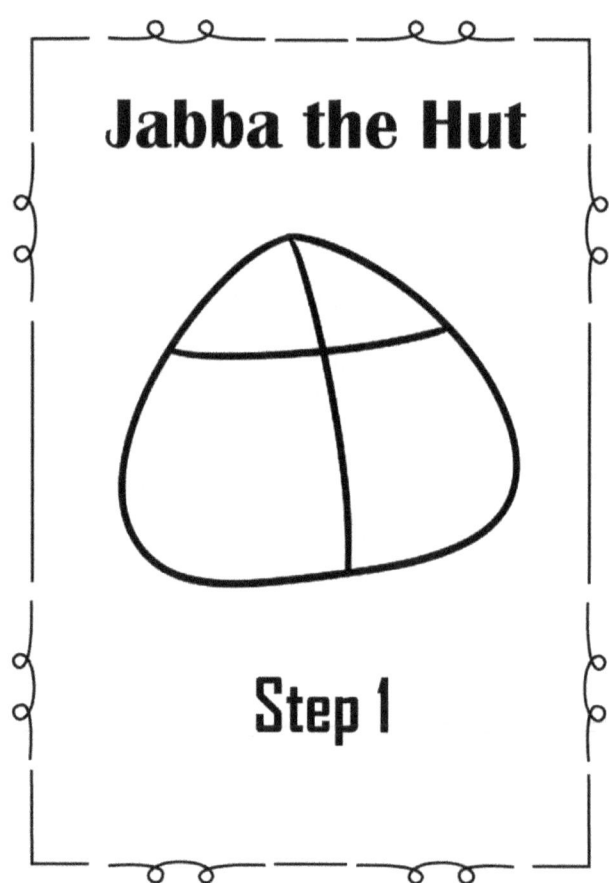

Step 1

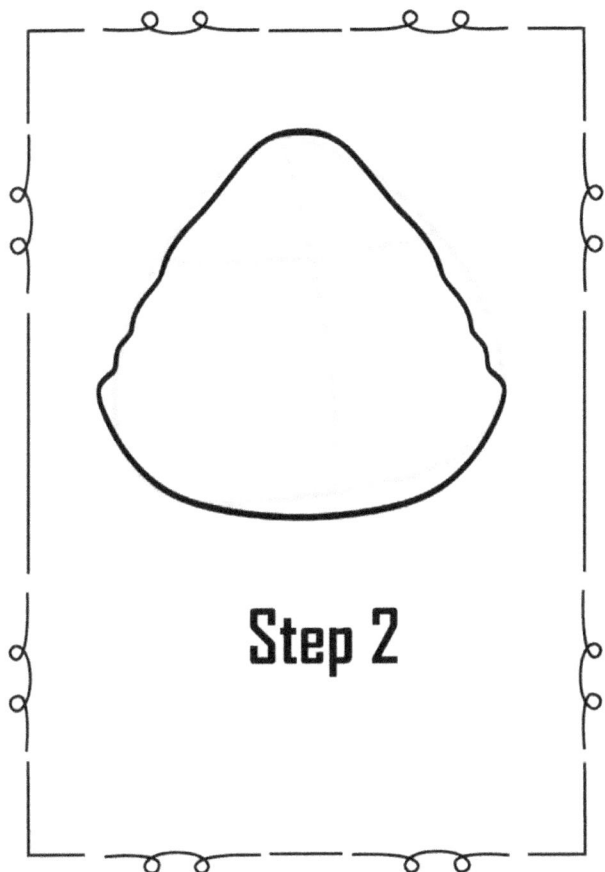

Step 2

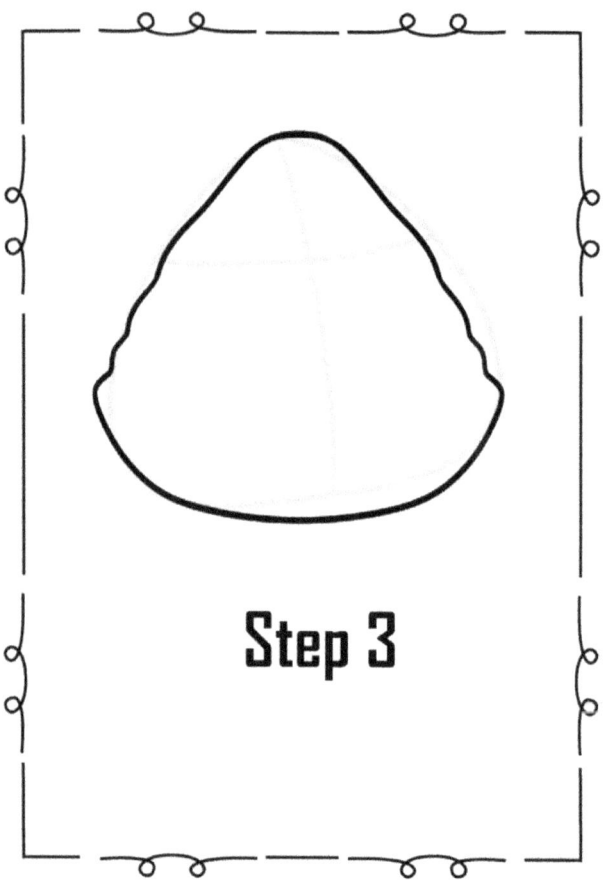

Step 3

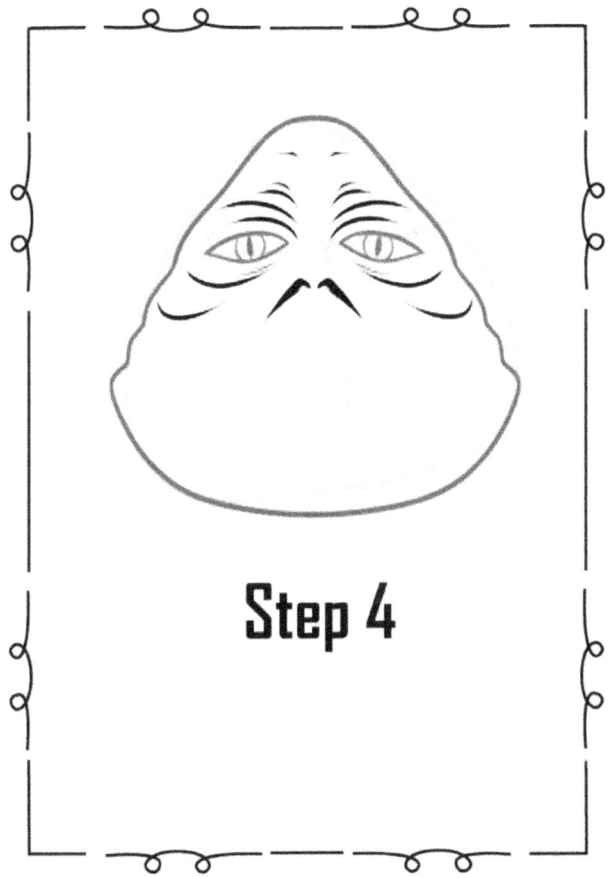

Step 4

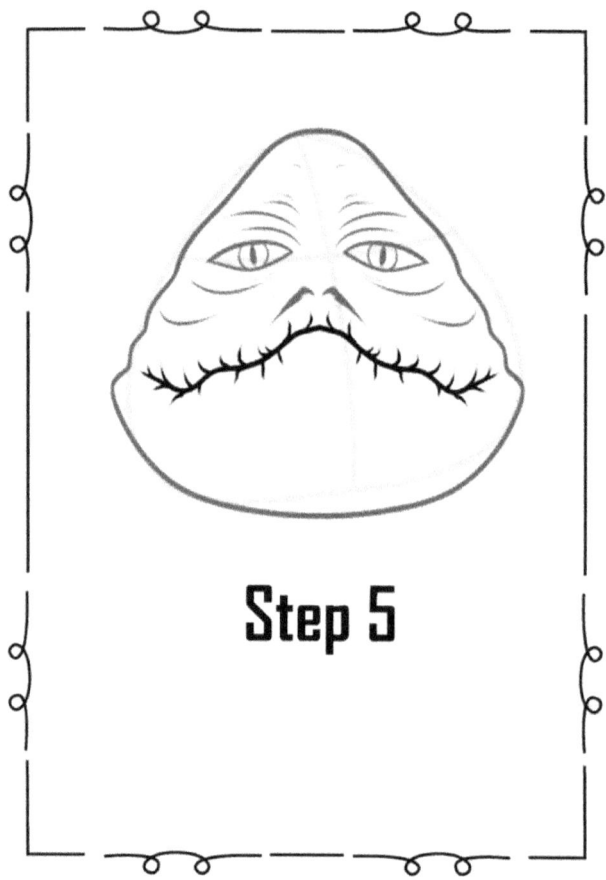

Step 5

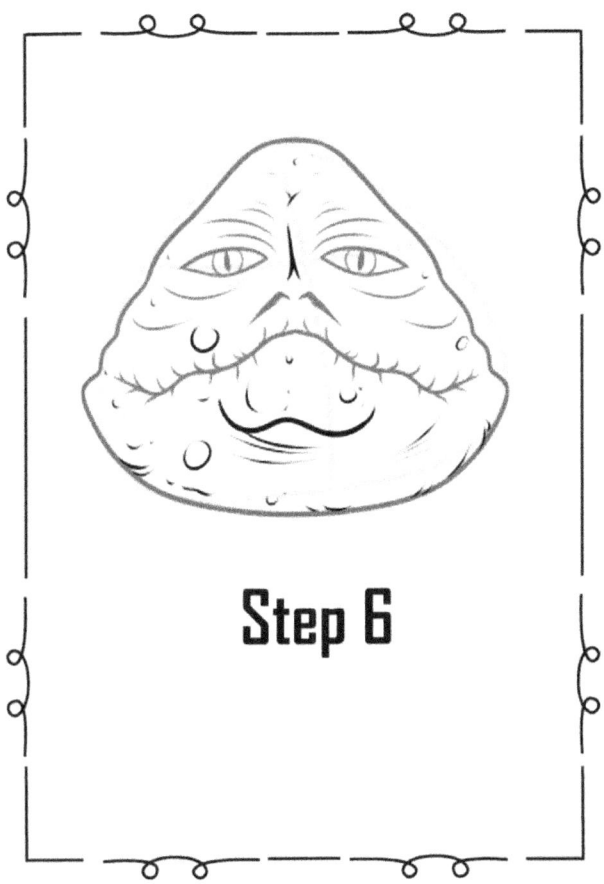

Step 6

Obi Wan Kenobi

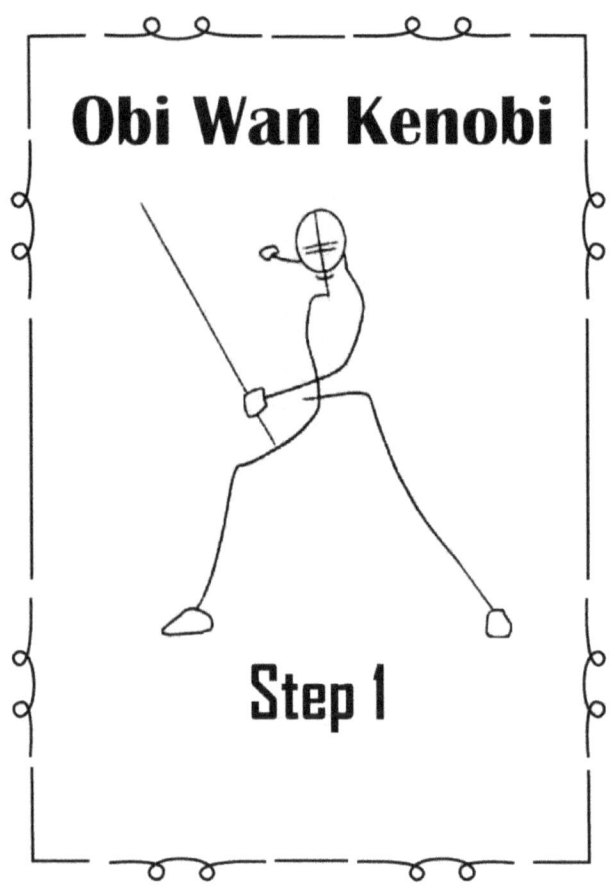

Step 1

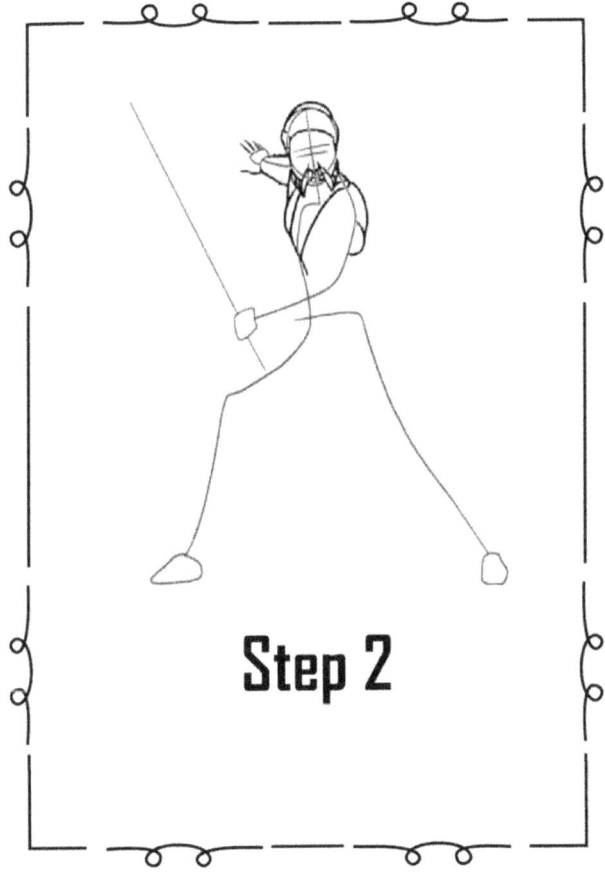

Step 2

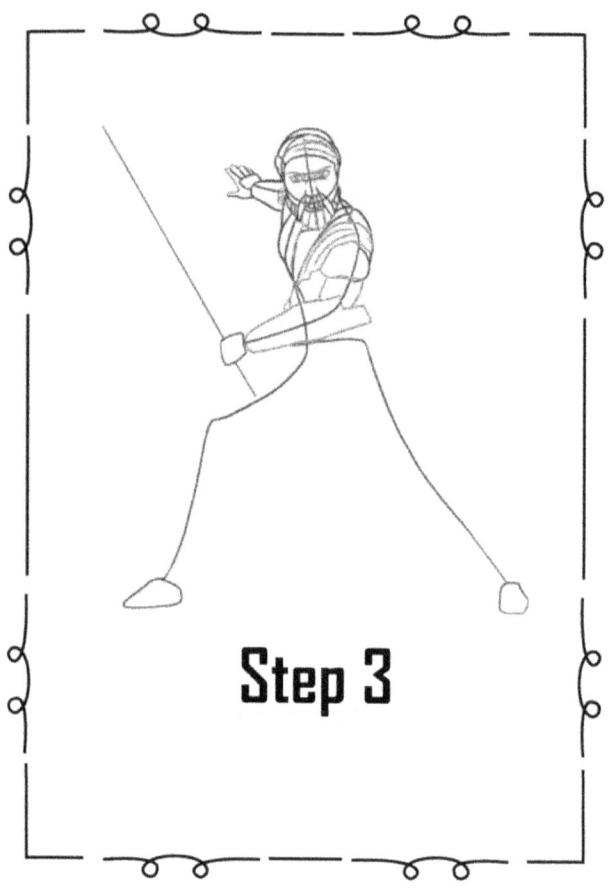

Step 3

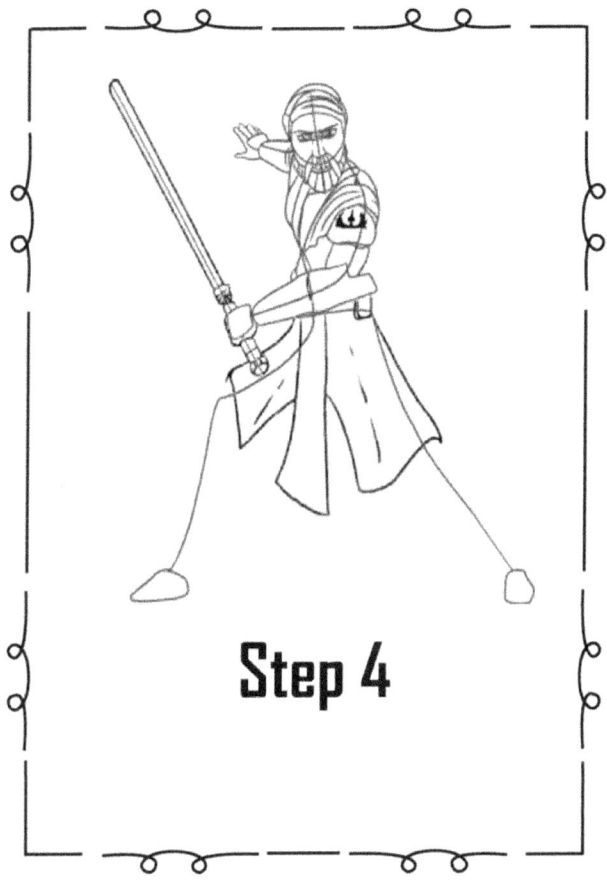

Step 4

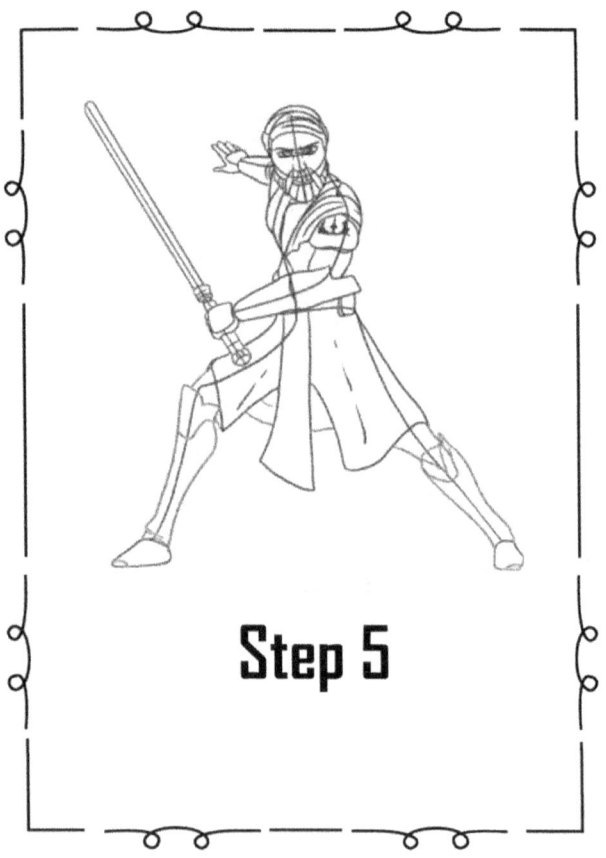

Step 5

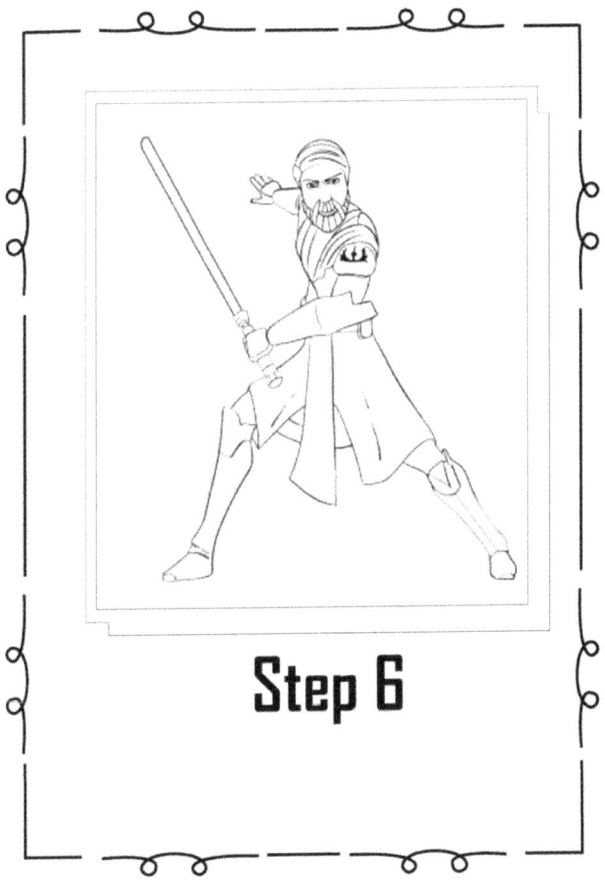

Step 6

R2 D2

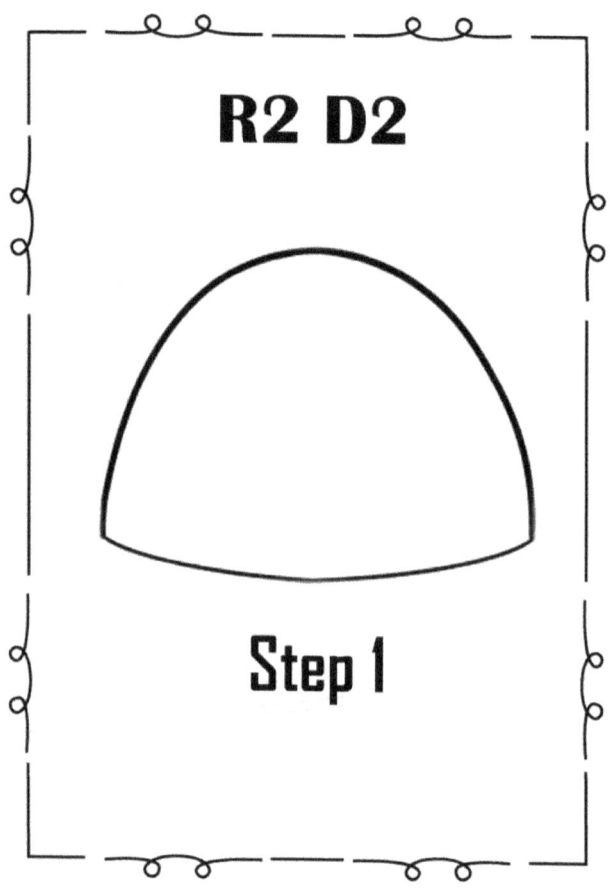

Step 1

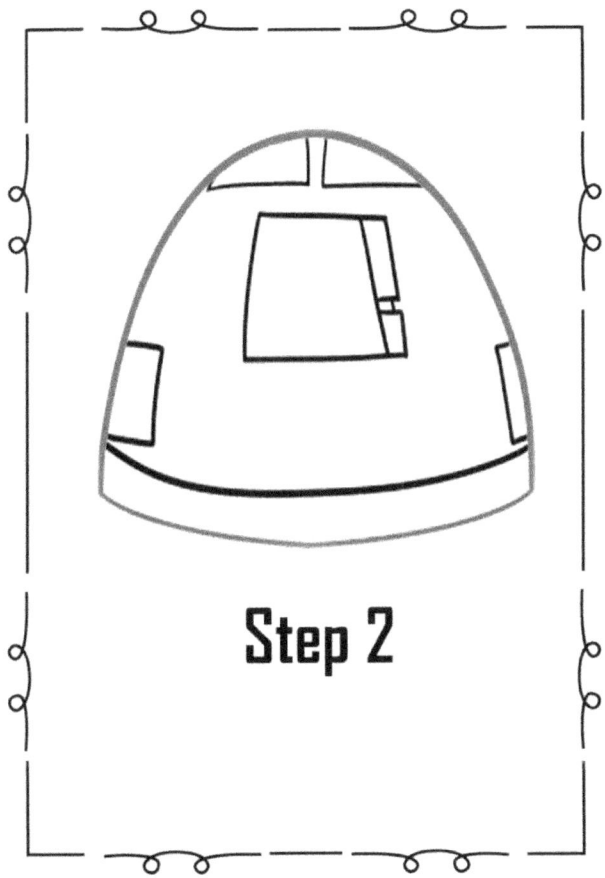

Step 2

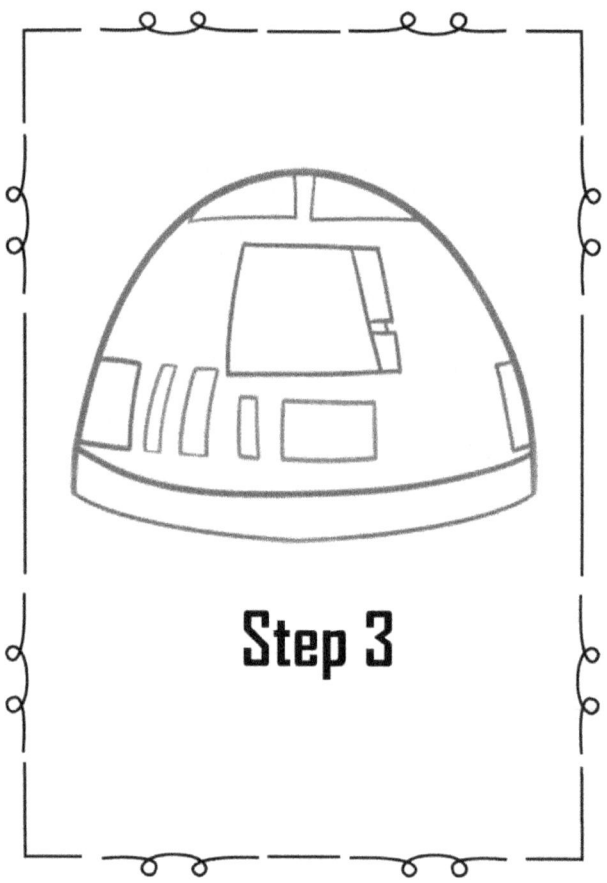

Step 3

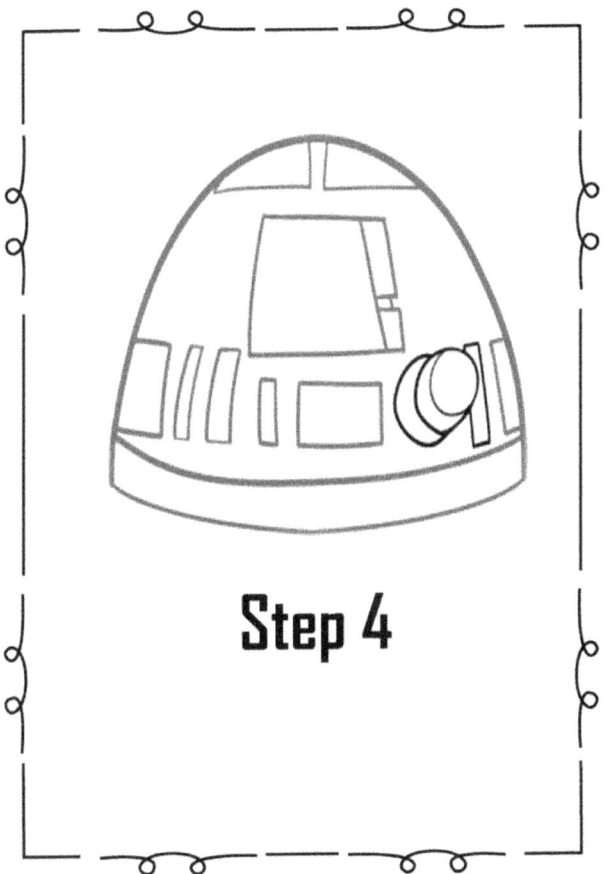

Step 4

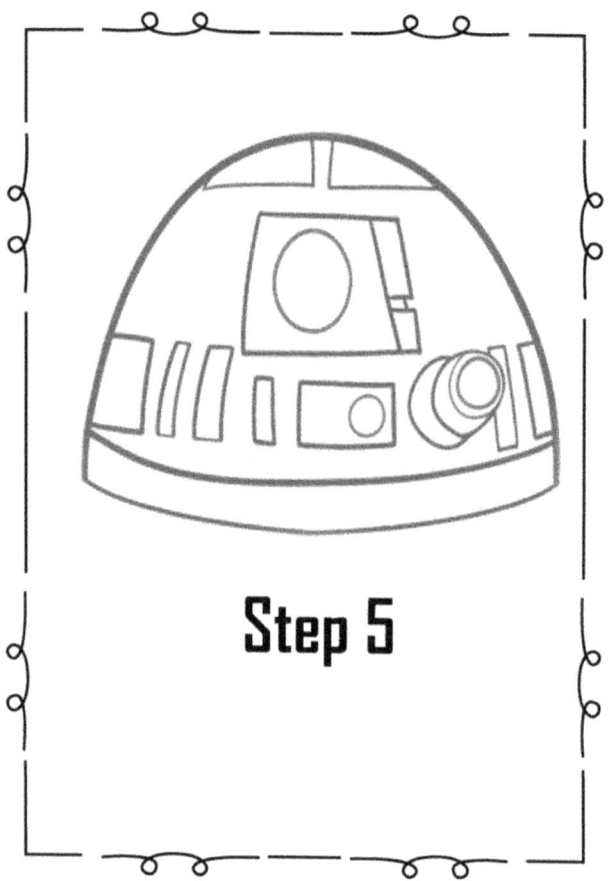

Step 5

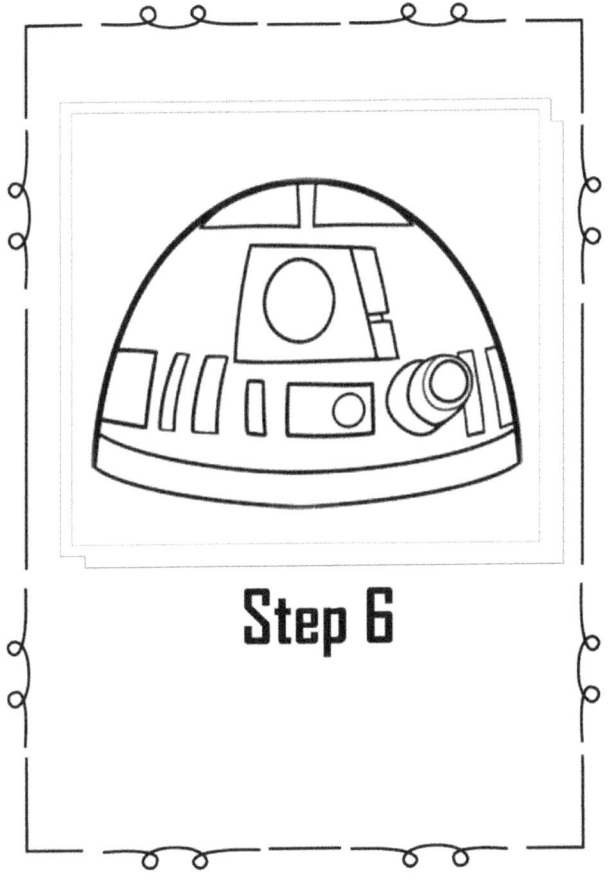

Step 6

The Head of Darth Maul

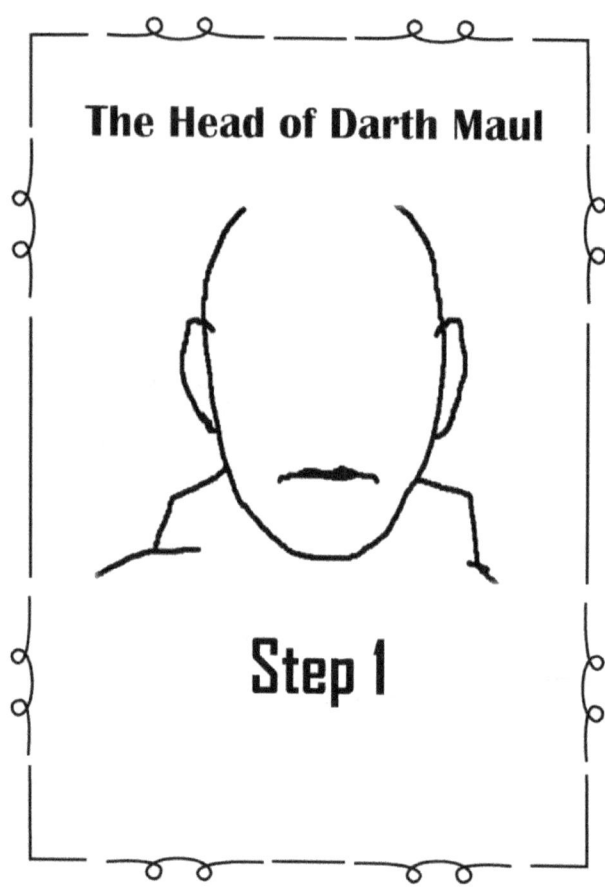

Step 1

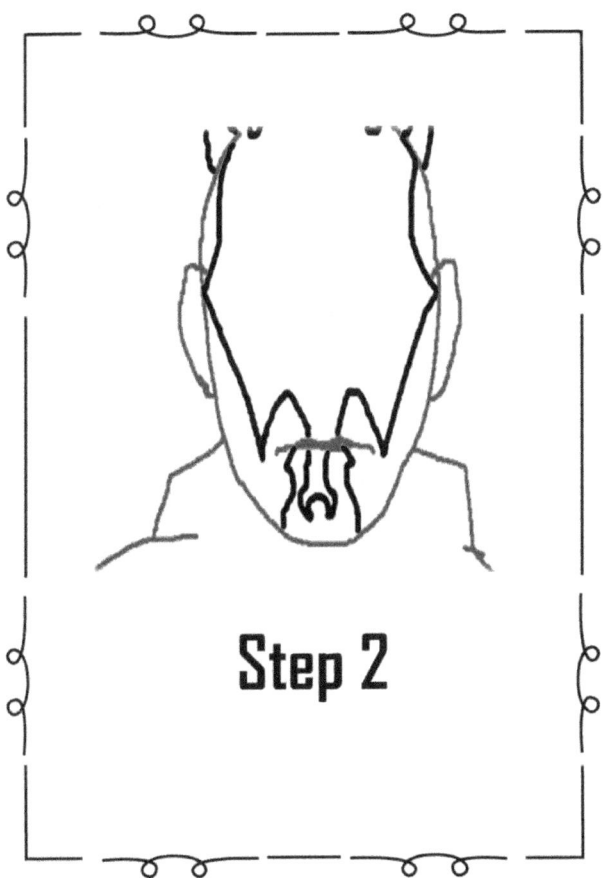

Step 2

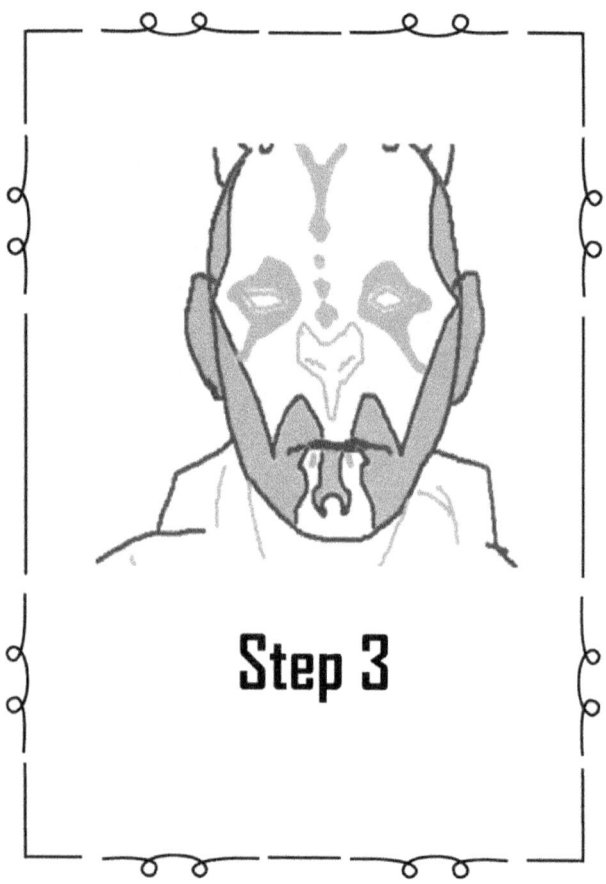

Step 3

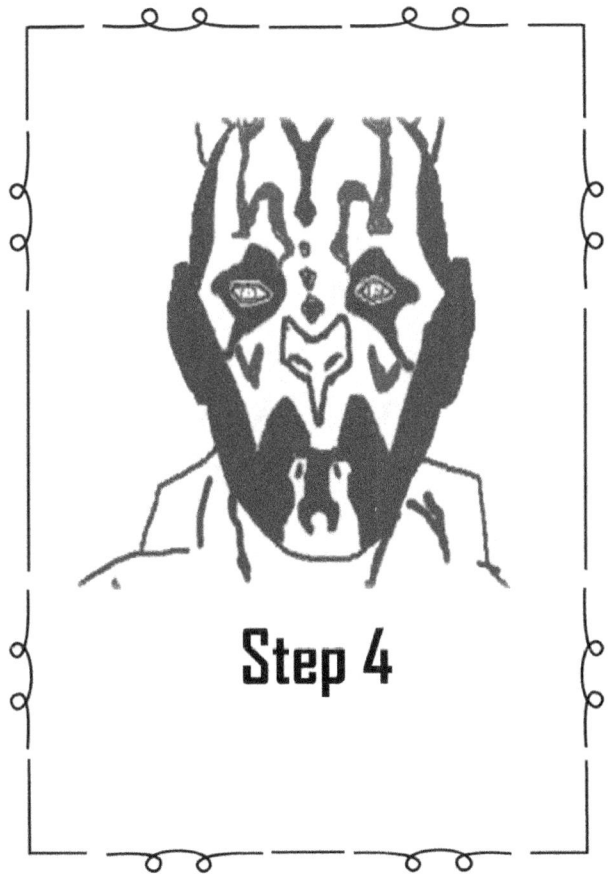

Step 4

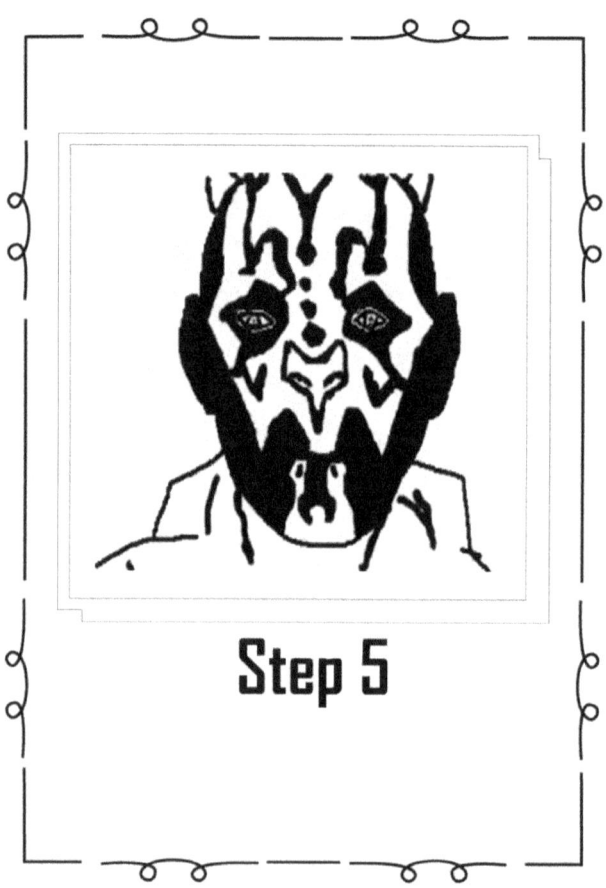

Step 5

Darth Sidious

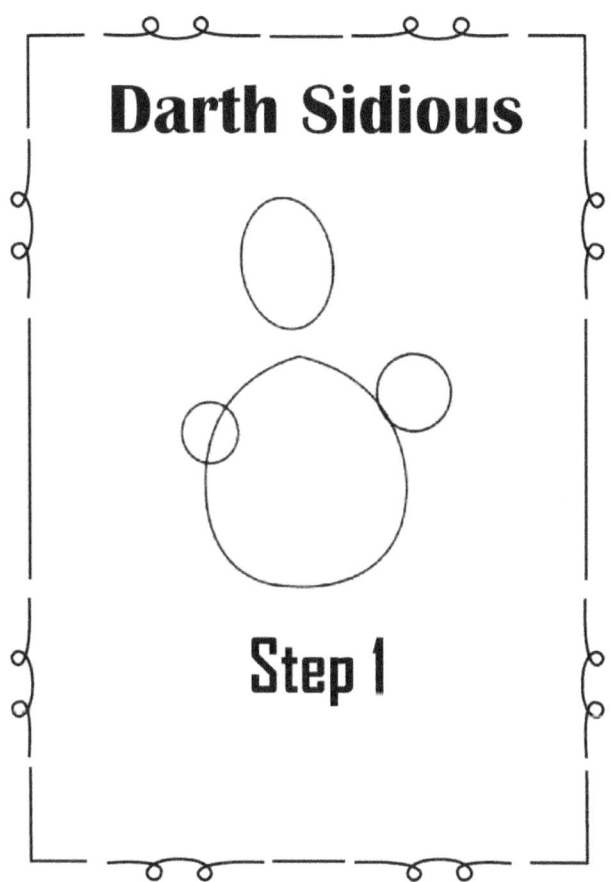

Step 1

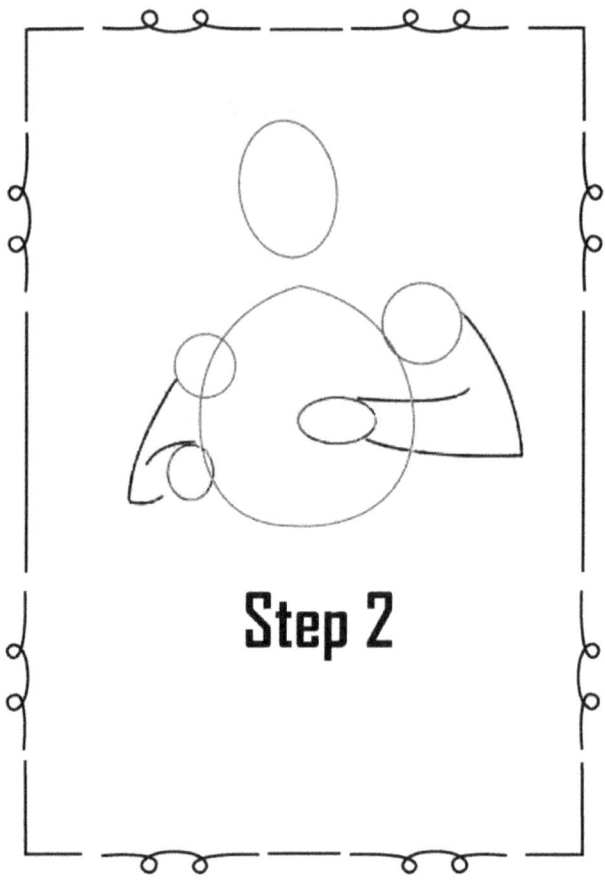

Step 2

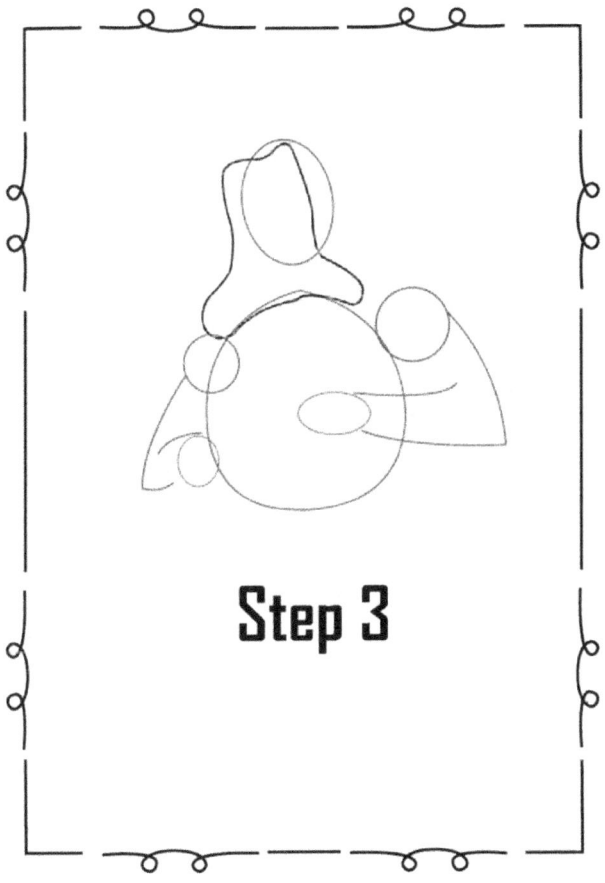

Step 3

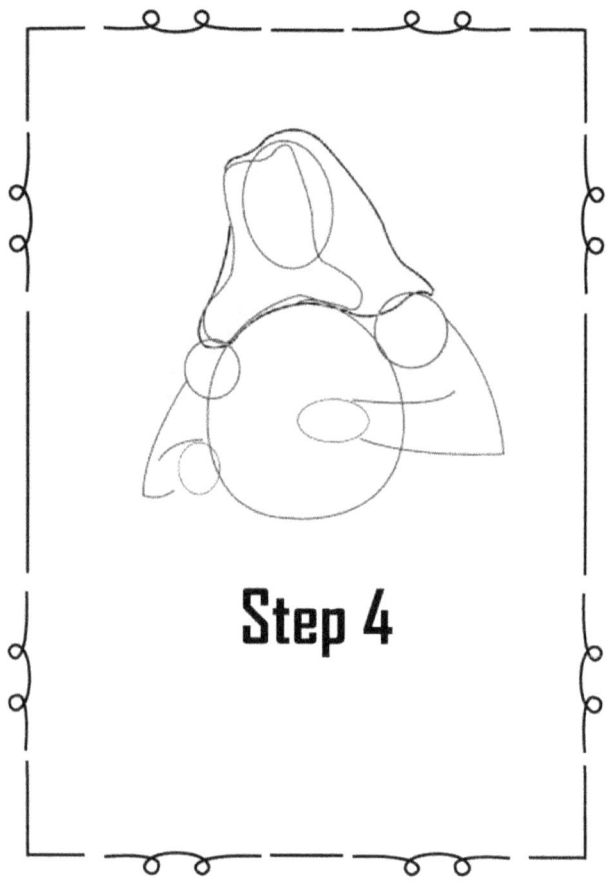

Step 4

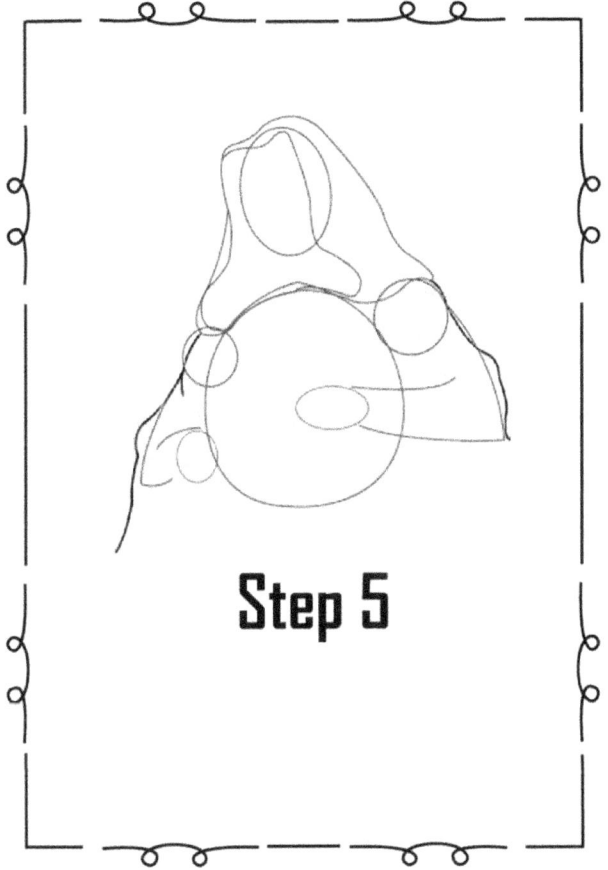

Step 5

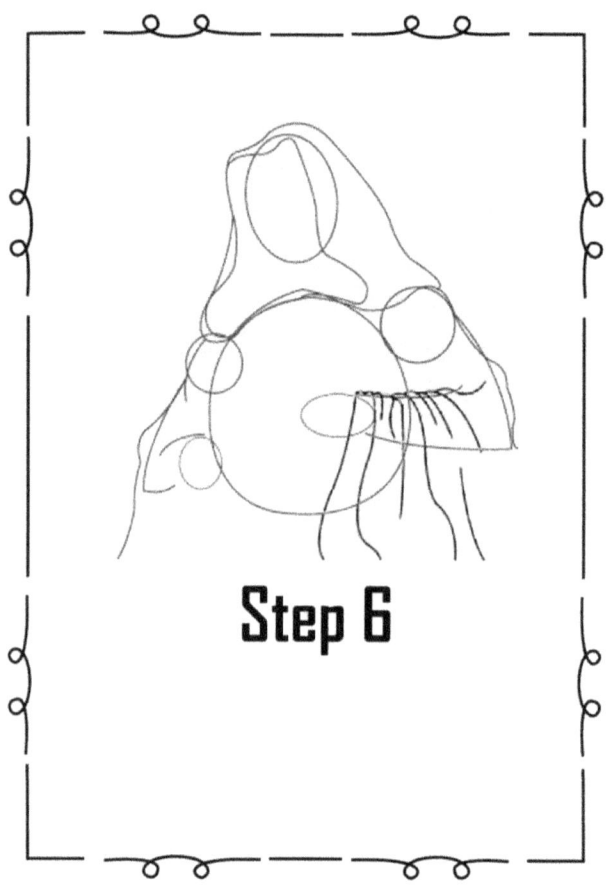

Step 6

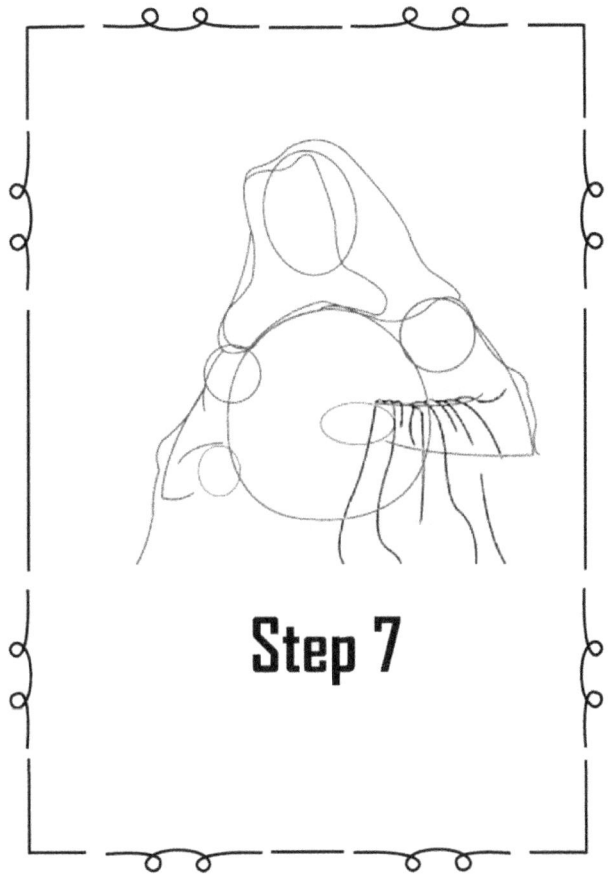

Step 7

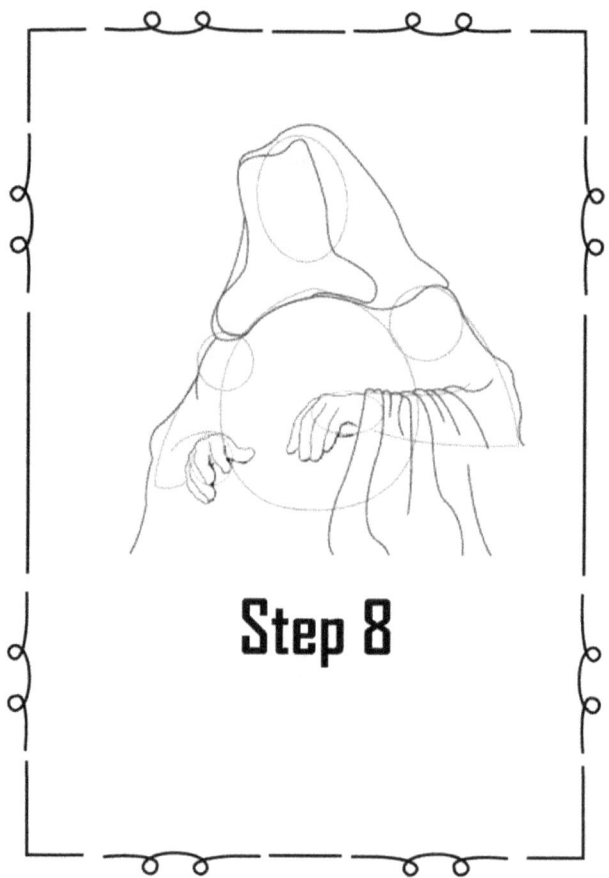

Step 8

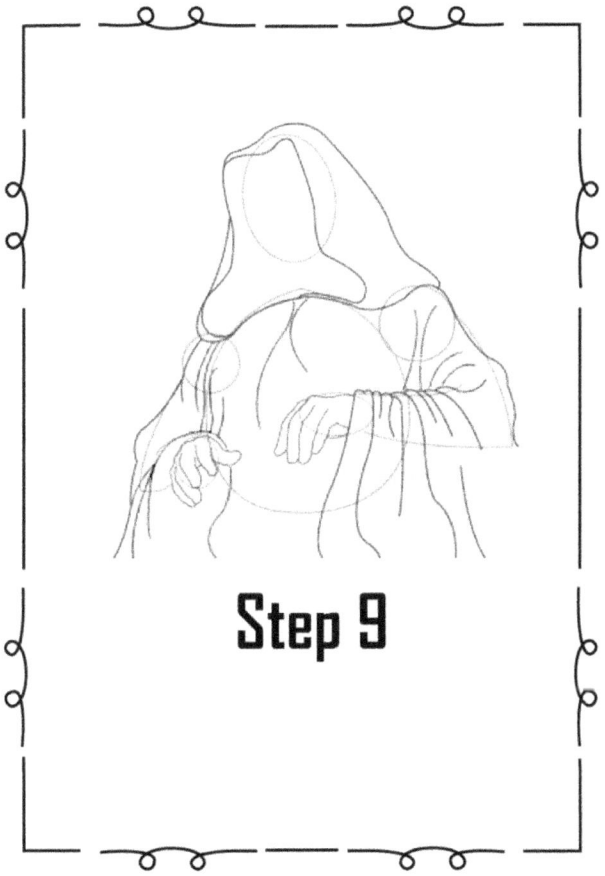

Step 9

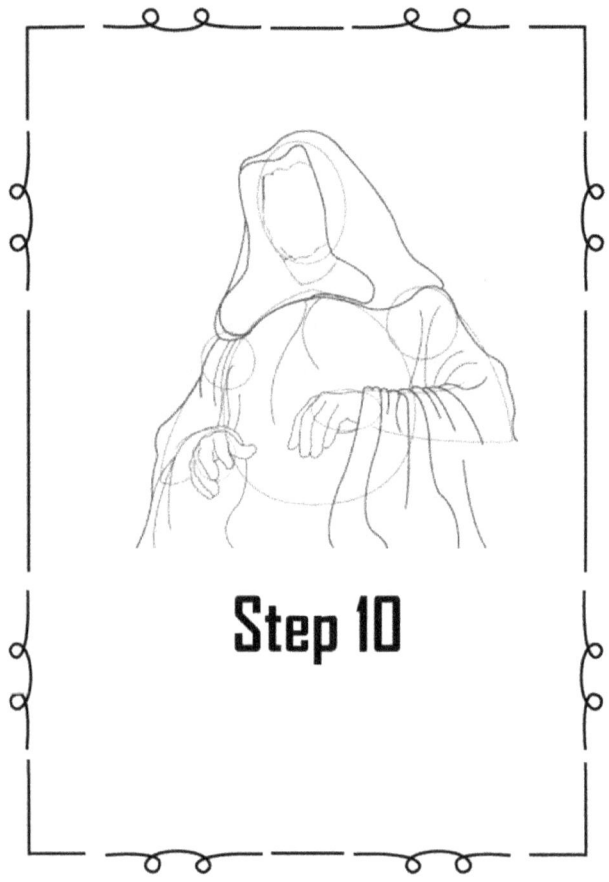

Step 10

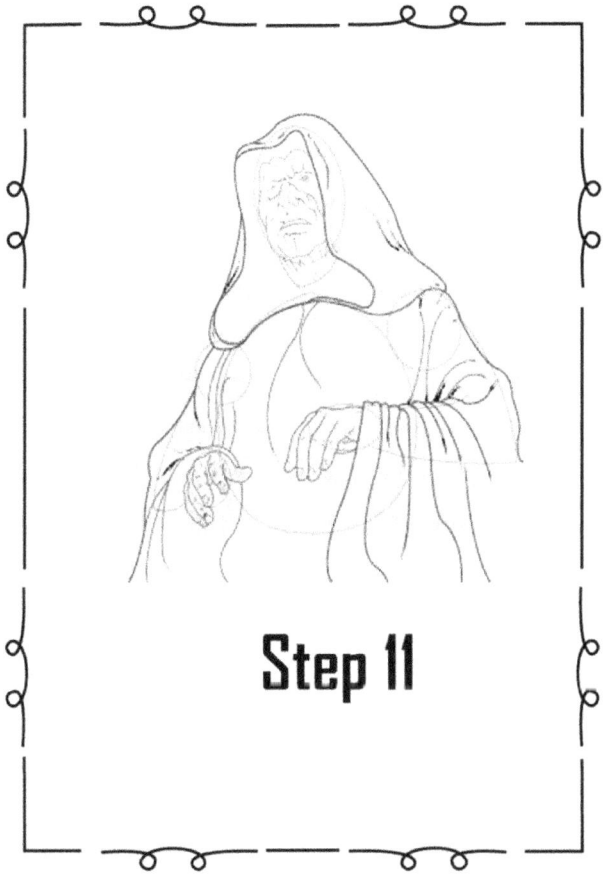

Step 11

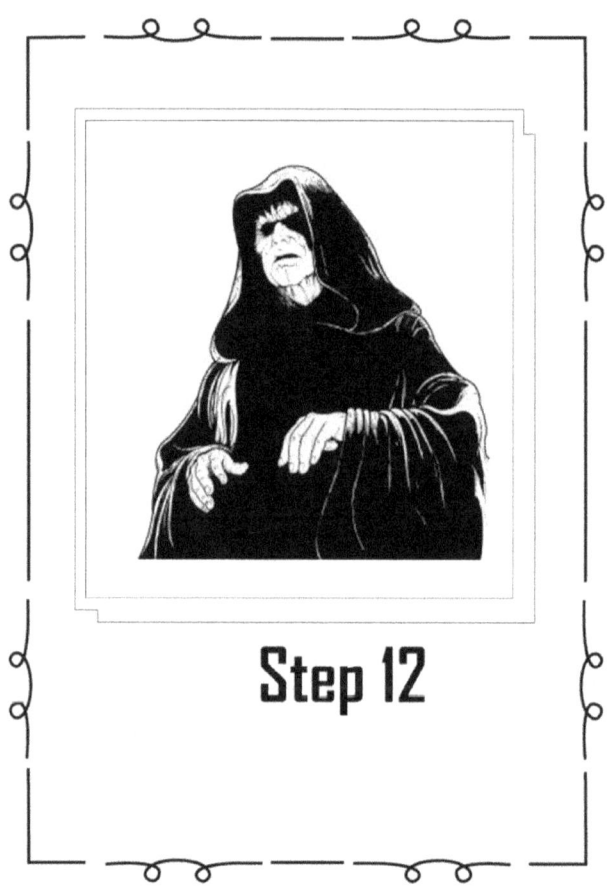

Step 12

Kylo Ren

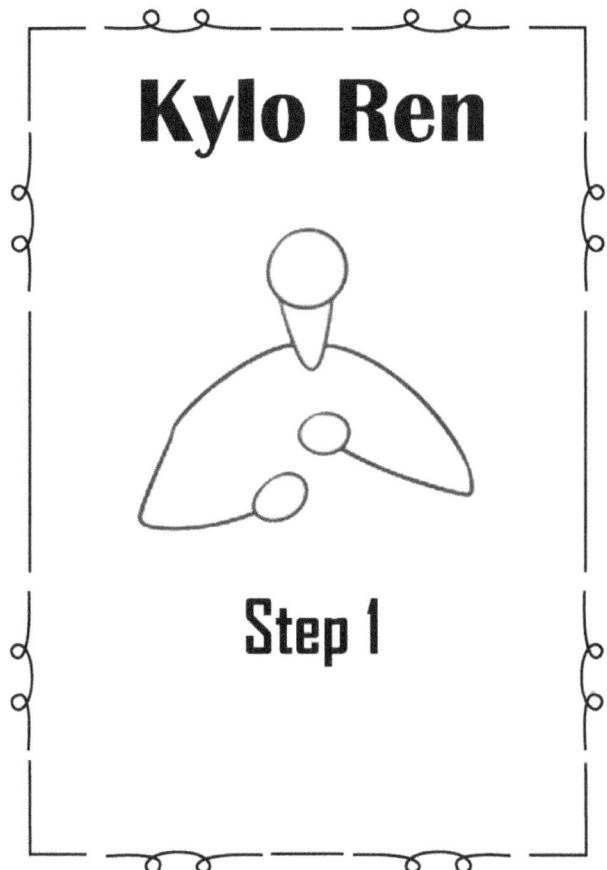

Step 1

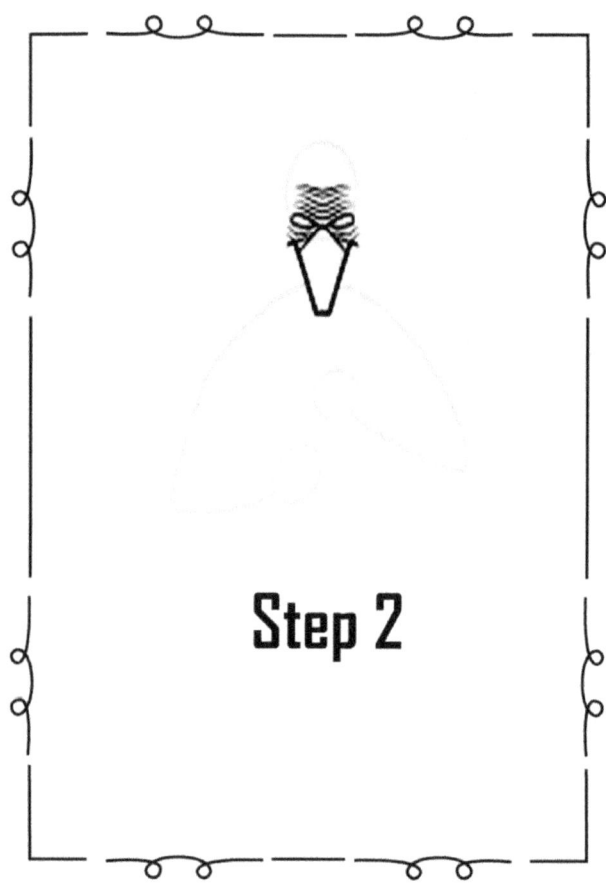

Step 2

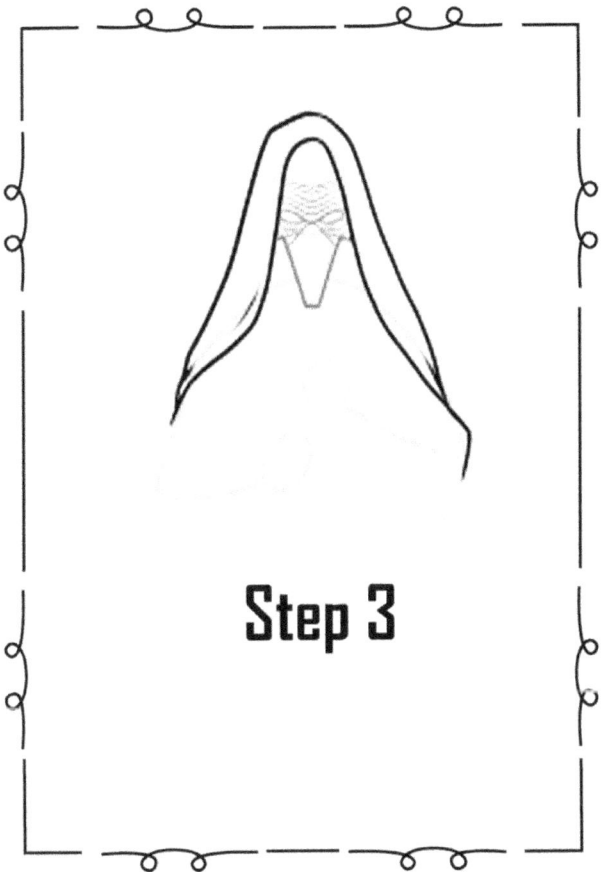

Step 3

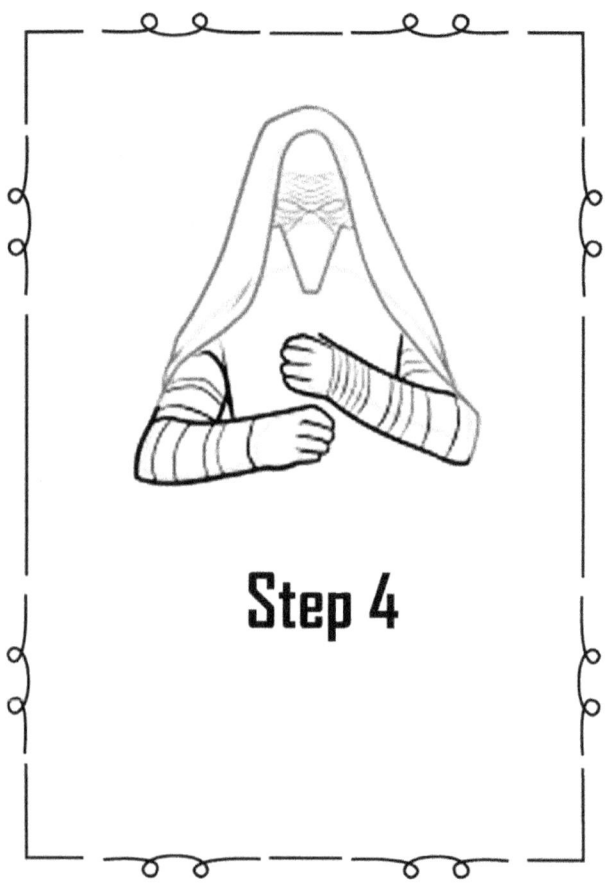

Step 4

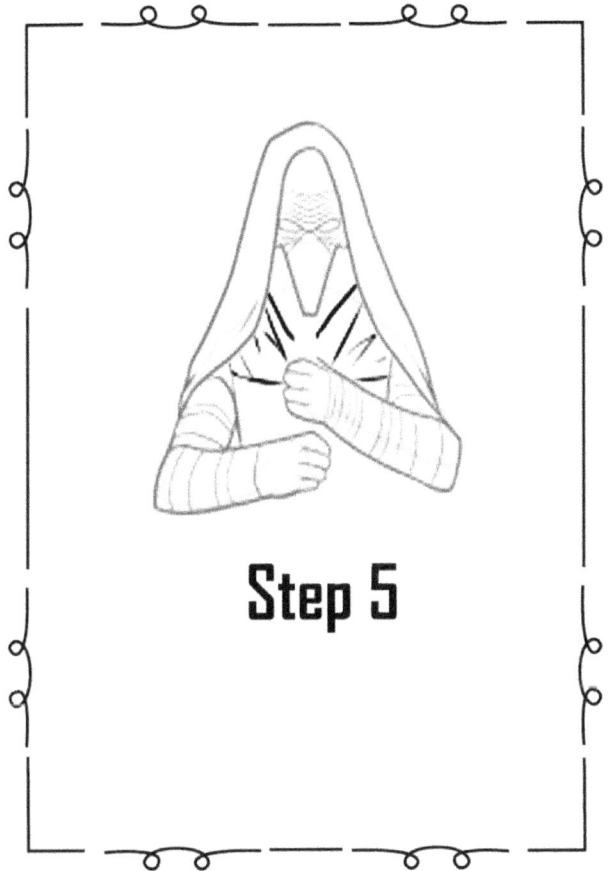

Step 5

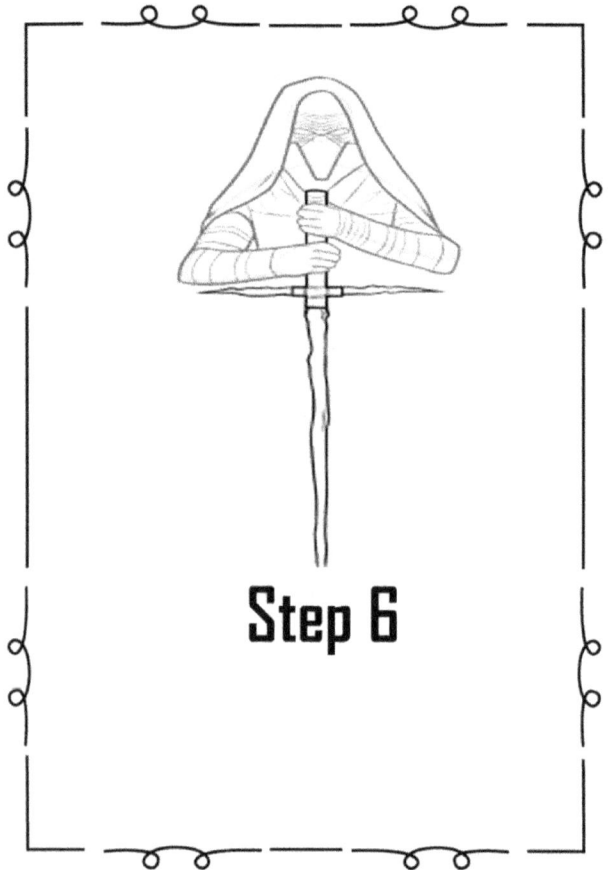

Step 6

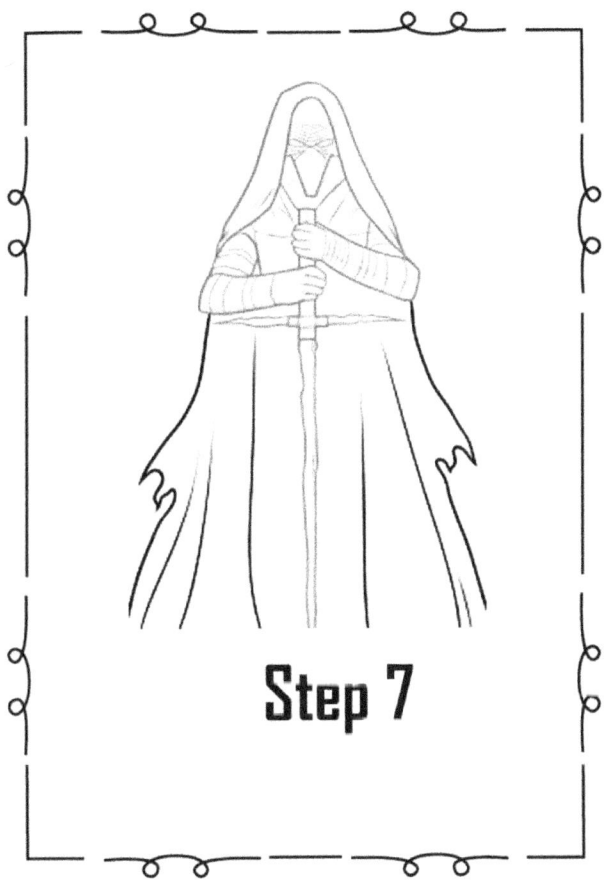

Step 7

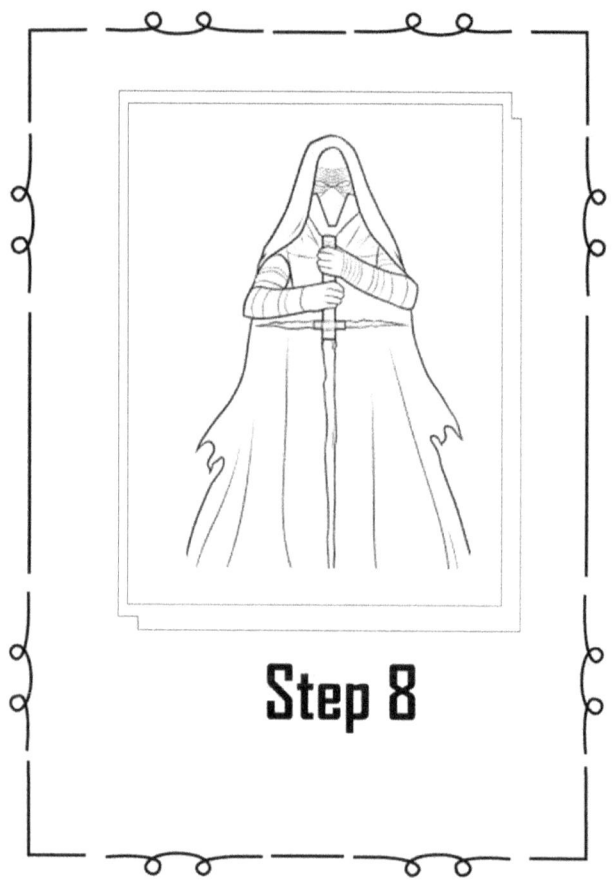

Step 8

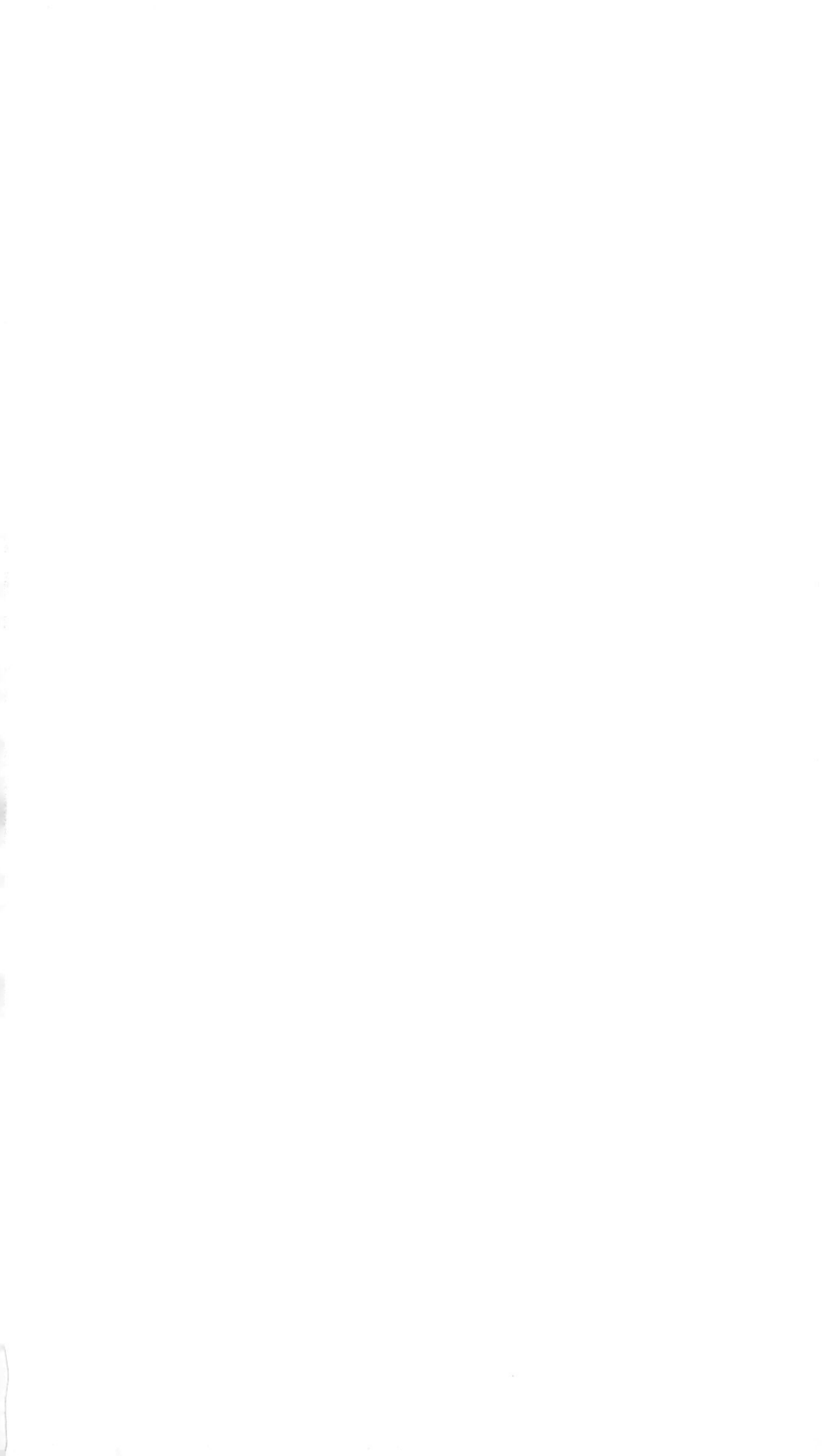